STECK-VAUGHN

America's Story

BOOK ONE ▪ TO 1865

Vivian Bernstein

Steck-Vaughn
Company

A Subsidiary of National Education Corporation

ABOUT THE AUTHOR

Vivian Bernstein has been a teacher in the New York City Public School System for a number of years. She received her Master of Arts degree from New York University. Bernstein is active with professional organizations in social studies, education, and reading. She is the author of *World History and You, World Geography and You* and *Health and You.*

ACKNOWLEDGMENTS

Pages 2–3: Illustrations from *Indians* by Edwin Tunis. Copyright© 1959 by Edwin Tunis. Used by permission of Thomas Y. Crowell Co. Originally published by the World Publishing Company. **Page 4:** National Collection of Fine Arts, Smithsonian Institution. **Page 9:** Library of Congress. **Page 12:** Chase Manhattan Bank. **Pages 13–14, 18–19:** Library of Congress. **Page 20:** The Bettmann Archive. **Page 23:** Jamestown Festival Park. **Page 24:** From *A History of the United States of America,* by Charles A. Goodrich, 1833. **Page 30:** Upper, From *Narrative and Critical History of America,* by Justin Windsor, 1884; Lower, Chicago Historical Society. **Page 32:** Upper, Courtesy, Mr. August A. Busch, Jr.; Lower, From *History of Alabama,* by William Garrot Brown, 1900. **Page 36:** Culver Pictures, Inc. **Page 37:** The Bettmann Archive. **Pages 42–43:** From *Dictionary of American Portraits.* **Page 42:** Library of Congress. **Page 44:** Top, Brown Brothers; Upper left, Library of Congress; Lower left, American Jewish Archives. **Page 48:** Upper, National Archives; Lower, Library of Congress. **Page 49:** Wide World Photos. **Page 50:** The Supreme Court Historical Society. **Page 54:** Upper, From *The Story of Our Country,* by Cooper, Estill, and Lemon, 1903; Lower, The Bettmann Archive. **Page 55:** The Bettmann Archive. **Page 56:** Library of Congress. **Page 60:** Upper, The Brooklyn Museum, Dick S. Ramsay Fund; Lower, Mount Vernon Ladies' Association. **Page 61:** Upper, Mount Vernon Ladies' Association; Lower, New York State Historical Association, Cooperstown. **Page 63:** From *Dictionary of American Portraits.* **Page 66:** Upper, State Historical Society of Missouri; Lower, Chicago Historical Society. **Page 68:** State Historical Society of Missouri. **Page 73:** Upper, Museum of the City of Mobile; Lower, Mariner's Museum. **Page 74:** Library of Congress. **Page 75:** Upper, Smithsonian Institution; Lower, From *Dictionary of American Portraits.* **Page 76:** Library of Congress. **Page 79:** Alabama Department of Archives and History. **Pages 80, 81** Upper: From *Indians of North America,* by Thomas L. McKenny and James Hall. **Page 81** Lower: Woolaroc Museum, Bartlesville, Oklahoma. **Page 82:** Library of Congress. **Page 85:** Upper, Mt. Holyoke College Library; Lower, Used with permission of Macmillan Publishing Co., from *Our Free Nation* by Edna McGuire and Thomas B. Portwood. Copyright © 1954, 1959, 1961, Macmillan Publishing Co., Inc. **Page 86:** Mt. Holyoke College Library. **Page 90:** Painting by Louis Eyth, Texas State Capitol. **Page 91:** Library of Congress. **Page 92:** Upper left, Painting by Dee Hernandez, Navarro Elementary School, San Antonio, Texas; Lower left, Texas State Library, Archives Division; Bottom, Painting by Cliff Young. **Page 93:** Upper, Library of Congress; Lower, University of Texas at Austin, Barker Texas History Center. **Page 96:** Texas Memorial Museum. **Page 97:** Chicago Historical Association. **Page 103:** Culver Pictures. **Page 105:** Reproduced by permission of the publisher from *United States History,* by Gavian and Hamm,© 1960 by D.C. Heath and Company, Lexington, Massachusetts; National Gallery of Art. **Page 106:** History Division, Los Angeles County Museum of Natural History. **Page 109:** Upper, State Historical Society of Missouri; Lower, Courtesy of the New-York Historical Society, New York City. **Page 110:** State Historical Society of Missouri. **Page 111:** Library of Congress. **Page 115:** Upper, Museum of the City of Mobile; Lower, New York Historical Society. **Page 116:** Upper, Library of Congress; Lower, Chicago Historical Society. **Page 117:** Upper, Valentine Museum; Lower, Library of Congress.

Cover Credits:
U.S. flag © COMSTOCK/Michael Stuckey
Photo inset of H.M.S. Rose © Rob Burlinson

Staff Credits:
Senior Editor: Diane Sharpe
Project Editor: Athena O. Kildegaard
Cover Designer: Joyce Spicer
Art Director: Joyce Spicer

ISBN 0-8114-4183-0
Copyright © 1990 Steck-Vaughn Company.

CONTENTS

CHAPTER 1

The First Americans

New Words ☆ Asia ★ Alaska ★ Northwest ★ fishing ★ Southwest ★ Midwest ★ Great Plains ★ millions ★ buffalo ★ forests ★ metal ★ bow and arrow ★ proud

This book tells the story of our country. We call our country the United States of America. A long time ago, there were no people in America. The first people to come to America were the Indians. The Indians lived in America before other people came.

Thousands of years ago, the Indians lived in Asia. The Indians walked from Asia to Alaska! How did the Indians do this? Today we cannot walk from Asia to Alaska. Now there is water between Asia and Alaska. Thousands of years ago, there was land between Asia

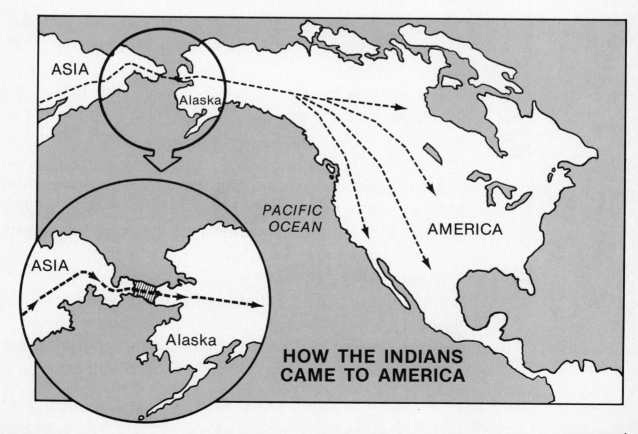

ASIA

Alaska

PACIFIC OCEAN

AMERICA

ASIA

Alaska

HOW THE INDIANS CAME TO AMERICA

1

The Indians of the Northwest sometimes trapped salmon fish in baskets and then caught them with spears.

AN INDIAN GIRL FROM THE SOUTHWEST

and Alaska. The Indians walked on this land into Alaska. The Indians walked south to the land we call the United States. The Indians lived in many parts of the United States.

The Indians moved to many places. The Indians did not have food stores. They always had to find their own food. Indian women always made clothes for their families.

Many Indians moved to the Northwest of the United States. In the Northwest, there were many fish in the oceans and rivers. The Indians of the Northwest went fishing to get food. They ate fish every day.

Some Indians moved to the Southwest. In the Southwest, there were few trees. There were very few fish and animals to eat. There was little rain. The Indians of the Southwest became farmers. They grew corn, beans, and cotton. They ate corn and beans. They made their clothes from cotton.

REGIONS OF THE
UNITED STATES

In the Midwest of the United States the land is very flat. We call this flat land the Great Plains. Millions of buffalo lived on the Great Plains. Many Indians lived on the Great Plains. These Indians became buffalo hunters. They ate buffalo meat.

In the East of the United States there were many forests. Many animals lived in the forests. Many Indians moved to these forests. These Indians became hunters. They killed deer and turkeys for food. They also became farmers. They grew corn and beans for their families.

All the Indians in America made their own tools. They needed tools for hunting, farming, and fishing. The Indians made their tools out of stones and animal bones. They did not make metal tools. They made knives out of stones. Indians hunted with bows and arrows. They did not have guns.

There are many Indians in the United States today. They still enjoy many songs, dances, and stories that their people enjoyed long ago. But Indians no longer live the way they did long ago. Indians now work at many kinds of jobs. There are Indian doctors and teachers. Some Indians are farmers and builders. The Indians today are proud that they were the first people to build our country. They are proud that they were the first Americans.

Indians who lived in the East killed deer and turkey for their food.

Indians living on the Great Plains hunted buffalo for their food and clothes.

USING WHAT YOU'VE LEARNED

★ Read and Remember

Finish Up ★ Choose a word in dark print to finish each sentence. Write the word on the correct blank.

Americans   stones   Asia   jobs   corn
fishing   hunters   East   buffalo

1. The Indians were the first _____.

2. The Indians walked from _____ to Alaska.

3. The Indians who lived in the Northwest went _____ for their food.

4. The Indian farmers of the Southwest grew beans and

_____.

4

5. Animals that lived on the Great Plains were the _____.

6. The Indians who lived on the Great Plains became _____.

7. Indians who lived in forests in the _____ became hunters.

8. The Indians made their tools out of animal bones and

_____.

9. Indians now work at many kinds of _____.

★ Think and Apply

Sequencing Events ★ Write the numbers **1, 2, 3,** and **4** next to these sentences to show the correct order. The first one is done for you.

_____ Today Indians are proud that they were the first Americans.

_____ The Indians walked from Asia to Alaska.

_____ Some Indians became hunters in the East of the United States.

__1__ The Indians lived in Asia.

★ Writing Workshop

Write four sentences that tell how the Indians lived in America. Use your own words. You may want to read the story again before you start writing.

_____

_____

_____

_____

_____

_____

_____

★ Crossword Puzzle

Each sentence below has a word missing. Choose the missing word for each sentence from the words in dark print. Then write the words in the right places on the puzzle.

ACROSS

stores   **metal**   **beans**
bones   **stone**   **Asia**

1. The Indians lived in _____ before they came to America.

2. The Indians made tools out of animal _____.

3. The Indians did not make _____ tools.

4. Indian knives were made of _____.

5. The Indians ate corn and _____.

6. The Indians did not have _____ where they could buy things.

DOWN

East   **Alaska**   **Southwest**
arrow   **hunter**   **farmers**

7. The Indians in the _____ were hunters and farmers.

8. People who grow vegetables for food are _____.

9. An Indian who killed animals for food was a _____.

10. Long ago there was land between Asia and _____.

11. The Indian hunter used a bow and _____.

12. The Indians of the _____ grew cotton so they could make clothes.

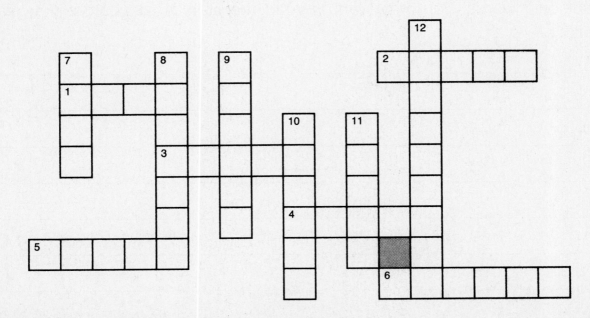

CHAPTER 2

Christopher Columbus

New Words ☆ Italy ★ Europe ★ India ★ jewels ★ spices ★ Africa ★ route ★ dangerous ★ Atlantic Ocean ★ Spain ★ Queen Isabella ★ discovered

CHRISTOPHER COLUMBUS

Christopher Columbus lived a long time ago. Columbus was born in 1451 in Italy. Columbus became a sailor. He also made maps.

A long time ago, everyone thought the world was flat. Most people in the world thought that there was no land between Europe and Asia. Only the Indians in America knew of their land.

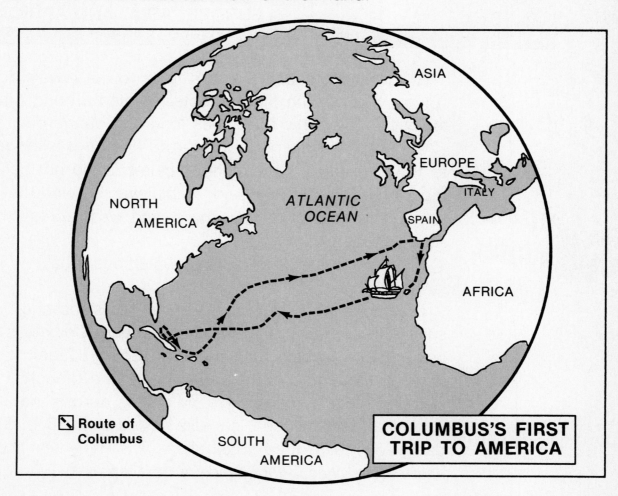

◤ Route of Columbus

COLUMBUS'S FIRST TRIP TO AMERICA

7

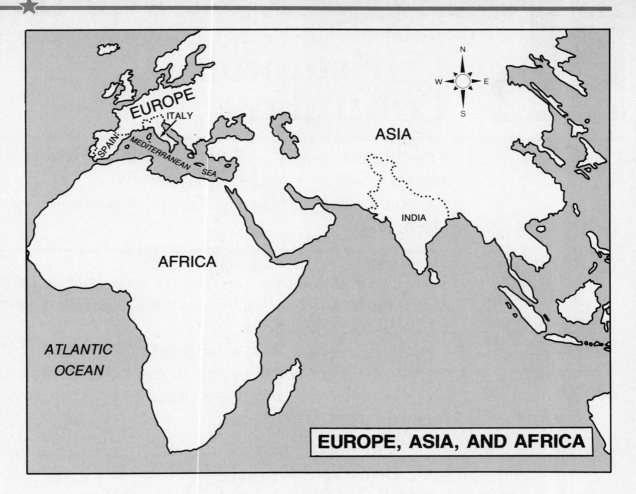

EUROPE, ASIA, AND AFRICA

At that time, people went to India to get jewels and spices. Most of the time, people traveled around Africa to reach India. This route was long and dangerous.

Christopher Columbus wanted to find an easier way to travel to India. Christopher Columbus did not believe the world was flat. He said, ''I believe the world is round. We can go to India by sailing west across the Atlantic Ocean.''

Many people did not believe Columbus. They laughed at him.

Columbus went to Spain. He needed ships and sailors to sail across the Atlantic Ocean. Columbus went to see Isabella, the queen of Spain. Queen Isabella thought Columbus was right. She thought Columbus could reach India by sailing across the Atlantic Ocean. Queen Isabella helped Columbus. She gave Columbus three small ships. The names of the ships were *Niña, Pinta,* and *Santa María.*

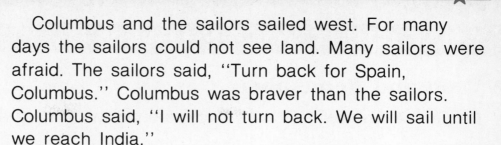

Columbus and the sailors sailed west. For many days the sailors could not see land. Many sailors were afraid. The sailors said, "Turn back for Spain, Columbus." Columbus was braver than the sailors. Columbus said, "I will not turn back. We will sail until we reach India."

On October 12, 1492, the sailors had not seen land for 33 days. On that day the three ships reached an island. This island was near the United States. The sailors were afraid no longer.

Columbus thought he was in India. He was not in India. Columbus was in America. People already lived on this island. Columbus called these people Indians because he thought he was in India. Now we call these people American Indians.

Today we say that Columbus discovered, or found, America in 1492.

After sailing for many days, Columbus finally reached an island near America.

USING WHAT YOU'VE LEARNED

★ **Read and Remember**

Circle the Answer ★ Draw a circle around the correct answer.

1. Where did Columbus want to go?

   America   India   Europe

2. Why did people want to go to India?

   to travel   to get jewels and spices   to see buffalo

3. What shape did Columbus believe the Earth was?

   round   flat   square

4. What did Queen Isabella give to Columbus?

   jewels   ships   spices

5. What ocean did Columbus sail across?

   Pacific Ocean   Indian Ocean   Atlantic Ocean

6. What did Columbus call the people he found in America?

   Indians   Americans   Asians

7. When did Columbus discover America?

   1492   1451   1412

★ **Skill Builder**

Using Map Directions ★ The four main directions are **north**, **south**, **east**, and **west**. On maps, these directions are shown by a **compass rose**.

You can also use the letters N, S, E, and W to show directions on a compass rose. Write the letters **N**, **S**, **E**, and **W** on the compass rose in the correct place. One is done for you.

Look back at the map on page 7. Then finish each sentence with the word **north, south, east,** or **west.**

1. Europe is _____ of the Atlantic Ocean.

2. North America is _____ of the Atlantic Ocean.

3. South America is _____ of North America.

4. Europe is _____ of Africa.

★ Think and Apply

Finding the Main Idea ★ A **main idea** is an important idea in the chapter. Less important ideas support the main idea. Read each group of sentences below. One of the sentences is a main idea. The other two sentences support the main idea. Write an **M** next to the sentence that is the main idea in each group. The first one is done for you.

1. _____ People wanted jewels from India.

   _____ People wanted spices from India.

   __M__ People sailed around Africa to get jewels and spices from India.

2. _____ The route to India was dangerous.

   _____ Columbus wanted to find a better route to India.

   _____ The route to India was very long.

3. _____ In 1492, Columbus sailed for many days to reach America.

   _____ Columbus sailed for 33 days.

   _____ Columbus had three ships, the *Niña,* the *Pinta,* and the *Santa María.*

4. _____ Columbus wanted to reach India.

   _____ No one in Europe knew about America.

   _____ When Columbus landed in America, he thought he was in India.

CHAPTER 3

The Spanish Explore America

New Words ☆ Spanish ★ Mexico ★ South America ★ Francisco Coronado ★ explored ★ Hernando de Soto ★ Florida ★ Mississippi River ★ Catholic ★ missions ★ Texas ★ California ★ New Mexico ★ priests ★ Santa Fé

SPANISH MONEY

Christopher Columbus discovered America for Spain in 1492. The Spanish king wanted people to live in America. Spanish people went to Mexico and South America. The king wanted his people to find gold in America. He wanted them to send the gold to Spain. He wanted Spain to be very rich.

Francisco Coronado lived in Mexico. Coronado wanted to find gold for Spain. He heard about seven cities that were made of gold. He thought he could find them in the United States. In 1540 Coronado and

For two years Coronado and his soldiers looked for gold.

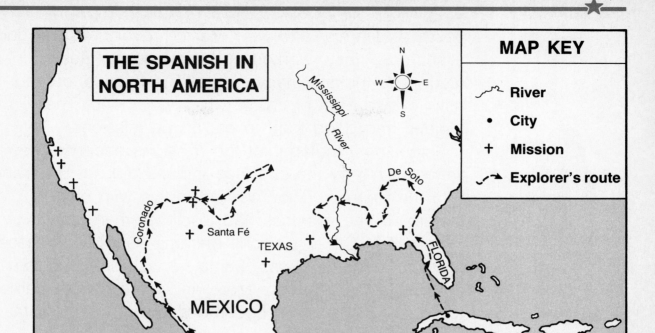

THE SPANISH IN NORTH AMERICA

MAP KEY

- ∿ River
- • City
- + Mission
- ⌇➤ Explorer's route

Mississippi River

Coronado

+ Santa Fé

TEXAS

De Soto

FLORIDA

MEXICO

HERNANDO DE SOTO

300 Spanish soldiers went to the Southwest of the United States. Coronado looked for gold in the Southwest for two years. Coronado found Indian farmers in the Southwest. He found Indian villages made of earth. But he never found the seven cities of gold. In 1542, Coronado went back to Mexico. Coronado had explored the Southwest. The king of Spain said that the Southwest of the United States belonged to Spain.

Hernando de Soto also wanted to find the seven cities of gold for Spain. De Soto went to Florida with more than 700 people in 1539. He looked for gold in the Southeast of the United States. While he was looking for gold, he came to a very big river. It was the Mississippi River. He was the first person from Europe to see this river. De Soto never found the seven cities of gold. The king of Spain said that Florida belonged to Spain, too.

The Spanish came to America to find gold. They did not find gold in the United States. Other Spanish people came to the Southwest of the United States. They wanted the Indians of the Southwest to become Catholics. That is why the Spanish built missions in

Texas, California, and New Mexico. Every mission had a church. Priests worked in the missions. Priests taught the Indians many things. The Indians learned how to take care of cows, pigs, and sheep. The Indians had good food to eat at the missions.

Sometimes, Indians left the missions because they were not happy there. These Indians did not like living with the Spanish. They wanted to live with other Indians. Some missions had to close when many Indians left. Other missions became very large. These missions became towns. Santa Fé was one Spanish mission in New Mexico. More and more people came to Santa Fé. Santa Fé became a town. Today Santa Fé is a city.

The Southwest and Florida belonged to Spain for 300 years. We can visit some of the old Spanish missions when we travel in the Southwest. Indians and Spanish priests do not usually live at the missions today. Many of our cities in the Southwest have Spanish names.

A SPANISH PRIEST

The Spanish built missions in the Southwest.

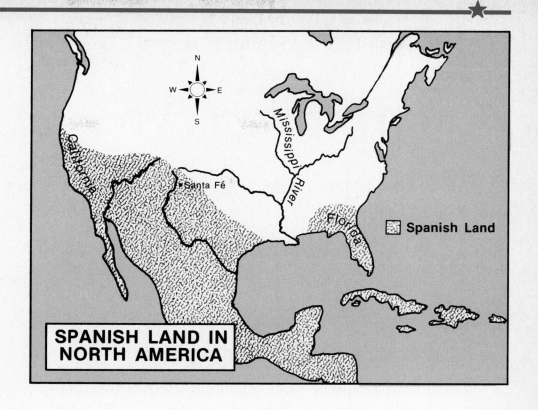

SPANISH LAND IN NORTH AMERICA

Spanish Land

USING WHAT YOU'VE LEARNED

★ Read and Remember

Finish the Sentence ★ Draw a circle around the word or words that finish each sentence.

1. The king of Spain wanted people to find _____.

   gold   food   buffalo

2. Coronado explored the _____ of the United States.

   Northwest   Southwest   Southeast

3. De Soto looked for gold in the _____.

   Northwest   Southwest   Southeast

4. De Soto was the first person from Europe to see the _____.

   Atlantic Ocean   Southeast   Mississippi River

5. Coronado and de Soto tried to find the _____ cities of gold.

   five   six   seven

6. The Spanish built _____ for the Indians.

farms   stores   missions

7. _____ learned how to take care of cows, pigs, and sheep.

Coronado   De Soto   The Indians

True or False ⋆ Write **T** next to each sentence that is true. Write **F** next to each sentence that is false.

_____ 1. The Spanish king said that Florida belonged to Spain.

_____ 2. The Spanish wanted the Indians to become Catholics.

_____ 3. The Spanish found a lot of gold in the United States.

_____ 4. Coronado found Indians in the Southwest.

_____ 5. The Spanish built missions for the Indians.

_____ 6. None of the missions had churches.

_____ 7. Santa Fé was a Spanish mission.

★ Think and Apply

Making Comparisons ⋆ Read each sentence below. Decide whether it tells about Coronado's trip or about de Soto's trip. Write a **C** next to each sentence about Coronado's trip. Write a **D** next to each sentence about de Soto's trip.

1. _____ This trip was to Florida.

2. _____ This trip was in the Southwest of the United States.

3. _____ More than 700 people went on this trip.

4. _____ There were 300 soldiers on this trip.

5. _____ They found Indian villages made of earth on this trip.

6. _____ On this trip, the Mississippi River was first seen by someone from Europe.

7. _____ After this trip Florida belonged to Spain.

16

★ Skill Builder

Using Map Keys ★ Maps often show many things. Sometimes maps use little drawings to show what something on the map means. A **map key** tells what those drawings mean. Look at the map key below. Write what each drawing means on the blanks of the map key.

MAP KEY	
〰 River	+ 1. _____
• City	• 2. _____
+ Mission	⌒� 3. _____
〰➤ Explorer's route	〰 4. _____

Use the map and map key on page 13 to finish these sentences. Circle the number or word that finishes each sentence.

1. There are _____ missions on this map.

    12   10   40

2. There were _____ missions in the west of the United States.

    7   15   25

3. There is _____ river on this map.

    1   2   3

4. De Soto's route began in the _____.

    east   north   west

5. Coronado's route began in the _____.

    north   west   east

CHAPTER 4

The First Thanksgiving

New Words ☆ Pilgrims ★ England ★ Holland ★ freedom of religion ★ Dutch ★ English ★ *Mayflower* ★ Massachusetts ★ Plymouth ★ terrible ★ hungry

A long time ago the Pilgrims lived in England. All the people in England had to pray in the king's church. The Pilgrims did not like the king's church. They wanted to pray in their own church.

The Pilgrims left England and went to a small country called Holland. There was freedom of religion in Holland. Freedom of religion means that all people can pray the way they want to pray. The Pilgrims could pray in their own church in Holland.

The Pilgrims landed after many months at sea. They were glad to reach their new home.

The Pilgrims first built a church. Then they built houses.

The people of Holland are called the Dutch. They speak the Dutch language. The Pilgrims did not like living in Holland. They wanted to keep their English ways. They decided to go to America where they could live as they wanted and have freedom of religion.

In 1620, the Pilgrims left Holland for America. They had a ship. Their ship was the *Mayflower*. The trip was slow. The weather was rainy and cold. Many Pilgrims became sick.

The *Mayflower* landed in Massachusetts. The Pilgrims started a town called Plymouth. Find Massachusetts on the map on page 29. The first winter in Plymouth was terrible. Many Pilgrims died. There was little food.

The Indians helped the Pilgrims. They helped the Pilgrims hunt and fish. The Indians showed them how to plant corn. The Pilgrims built a church. Then the Pilgrims built houses.

The Indians and the Pilgrims had the first Thanksgiving in 1621.

By November 1621 the Pilgrims had a lot of food. They would not be hungry that winter. The Pilgrims were very happy.

The Indians and the Pilgrims had the first Thanksgiving in November 1621. The Pilgrims and the Indians had a party. The Pilgrims gave thanks to God for helping them. They said "thank you" to the Indians for helping them. This was the first Thanksgiving in America.

USING WHAT YOU'VE LEARNED

★ Read and Remember

Circle the Answer ★ Draw a circle around the correct answer.

1. Where did the Pilgrims first live?

   Holland   England   America

2. Where did the Pilgrims first travel?

   Holland   America   India

3. What was the name of the Pilgrims' ship?

   Niña   *Mayflower*   *Pinta*

4. Why did the Pilgrims come to America?

   to become farmers   to practice their religion

         to meet the Indians

5. What town in America did the Pilgrims start?

   Massachusetts   Plymouth   Boston

6. How did the Indians help the Pilgrims?

   taught them hunting and fishing   built their church

   ·   gave them a place to live

★ Think and Apply

Cause and Effect ★ A **cause** is something that makes something else happen. What happens is called the **effect**.

   CAUSE = The doorbell rang.
   EFFECT = Mr. Ruiz answered the door.

Read each pair of sentences below. Decide which one is the cause (what happens first). Decide which one is the effect (what happens next). Write **C** for cause or **E** for effect next to each sentence. The first one is done for you.

1. __C__ The Pilgrims had to pray in the king's church.
   __E__ The Pilgrims left England.

2. _____ The Pilgrims left Holland and went to America.
   _____ The Pilgrims couldn't keep their English ways in Holland.

3. _____ The long trip to America was rainy and cold.
   _____ Many Pilgrims got sick.

4. _____ Many Pilgrims died the first winter in America.
   _____ The Pilgrims had little food for the long, cold winter.

5. _____ The Pilgrims began growing corn.
   _____ The Indians showed the hungry Pilgrims how to grow corn.

6. _____ The Indians helped the Pilgrims get ready for the next winter.
   _____ The Pilgrims had a party to thank the Indians.

★ Writing Workshop

Write a paragraph telling why the Pilgrims gave thanks. Give at least three reasons why they were thankful.

_____

_____

_____

_____

_____

★ Crossword Puzzle

Each sentence below has a word missing. Choose the missing word for each sentence from the words in dark print. Then write each word in the right place on the puzzle.

ACROSS

Holland   Indians   Massachusetts

1. The Pilgrims and the _____ had the first Thanksgiving.

2. The Mayflower landed in _____.

3. There was freedom of religion in _____.

DOWN

Plymouth   fish   Dutch

4. The Pilgrims started a town called _____.

5. The people in Holland speak the _____ language.

6. The Indians helped the Pilgrims hunt and _____.

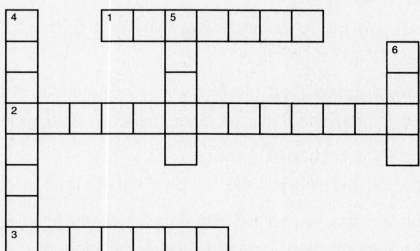

CHAPTER 5

The English Settle America

New Words ☆ settlers ★ Jamestown ★ Virginia ★ colony ★ Puritans ★ Roger Williams ★ Providence ★ Rhode Island ★ Anne Hutchinson ★ Maryland ★ Quakers ★ William Penn ★ Pennsylvania ★ James Oglethorpe ★ Georgia

AN ENGLISH SHIP

We learned that the Pilgrims came to America because they wanted freedom of religion. The Pilgrims were not the first group of English people to live in America. The first group of English people came to America in 1585, but their settlement failed.

In 1607 English settlers again came to America. They started a town called Jamestown. Jamestown was in the Virginia colony. A colony was land that England owned. The English did not come to Jamestown for freedom of religion. They came to Jamestown to find gold. The English did not find gold.

These homes are like the homes built by the first English settlers in Jamestown.

At first, the settlers did not want to work in Jamestown. They did not want to grow food or build houses. The settlers were very hungry during the first winter. Then they began to work hard. They built farms and houses. More people came to live in Jamestown. Most settlers did not return to England.

The Puritans were another group of people in England who did not want to pray in the king's church. In the year 1628, a group of Puritans came to America. Later, more Puritans came. The Puritans built towns in Massachusetts. Everyone in Massachusetts had to pray in Puritan churches. The Puritans did not let other people have freedom of religion.

Roger Williams lived with the Puritans. He was not happy in the Massachusetts colony. Roger Williams said, "Everyone should have freedom of religion. People should be able to pray in the church they want." Roger Williams left Massachusetts. Roger Williams started the city of Providence in Rhode Island. He started the Rhode Island colony in 1636. Providence was the first city in America where there was freedom of religion for all.

Roger Williams started the new colony of Rhode Island.

Anne Hutchinson left Massachusetts and started a new town in Rhode Island.

Anne Hutchinson was a woman who lived in Massachusetts. Anne Hutchinson thought all people should have freedom of religion. The Puritans wanted Anne Hutchinson to leave Massachusetts. She went to Rhode Island in 1638 and started a town. There was freedom of religion in Anne Hutchinson's town.

More and more English people came to America because they wanted freedom of religion. Catholic people did not have freedom of religion in England. In 1634, 300 Catholics came to America. They started a colony called Maryland.

The Quakers were another group of people who would not pray in the king's church. William Penn was a Quaker. In 1681 William Penn started the Pennsylvania colony. There was freedom of religion for everyone in Pennsylvania. The Indians liked William Penn. There was peace in the Pennsylvania colony.

In England there were some people who did not have any money. People who were in debt were put into jail. These people could not work or help

JAMES OGLETHORPE

their families. James Oglethorpe started the Georgia colony to help these people. In 1733 James Oglethorpe went to Georgia with 120 people. These people worked hard in Georgia. They started farms and built homes. Many poor people from Europe came to live and work in the Georgia colony.

Each year, more and more English people came to live in the colonies near the Atlantic Ocean. The map on page 29 is a map of the English colonies. By 1753 there were thirteen English colonies along the Atlantic Ocean.

USING WHAT YOU'VE LEARNED

★ Read and Remember

Write the Answer ★ Write a sentence to answer each question.

1. Why did the English come to Jamestown? _____

_____

2. Why did Roger Williams not like living with the Puritans in

Massachusetts? _____

_____

3. Why did Anne Hutchinson leave Massachusetts? _____

_____

4. Why did the Catholics come to America? _____

_____

5. Who started the Pennsylvania colony? _____

_____

6. Who did James Oglethorpe bring to Georgia? _____

_____

★ Think and Apply

Drawing Conclusions ★ Read the first two sentences below. Then read the third sentence. Notice how it follows from the first two sentences. It is called a **conclusion**.

> There was no freedom of religion in England.
> The Pilgrims wanted to pray in their own church.

CONCLUSION   The Pilgrims left England to find freedom of religion.

Read the first two sentences. Then look in the box for the conclusion you can make. Write the letter of the conclusion on the blank. The first one is done for you.

1. The settlers did not want to grow food.
   They did not build houses.

   Conclusion __d__

2. The Puritans did not let people have freedom of religion.
   Roger Williams wanted freedom of religion.

   Conclusion _____

3. The Puritans did not let people have freedom of religion.
   They did not like the way Anne Hutchinson wanted to change things.

   Conclusion _____

4. There was freedom of religion in Pennsylvania.
   The Indians liked William Penn.

   Conclusion _____

5. Many English people were in jail for debt.
   James Oglethorpe wanted to help these people.

   Conclusion _____

> a. They asked her to leave because of her ideas.
> b. He started a colony with people from English jails.
> c. He left Massachusetts to start his own colony.
> d. They were hungry and cold the first winter.
> e. The colony was very peaceful.

★ Skill Builder

Reading a Chart ★ A chart lists a group of facts. Charts help you learn facts quickly. Read the chart below to learn about the English colonies in America. Then answer each question.

Where was the colony?	Who started the colony?	When was the colony started?	Why was the colony started?
Providence, Rhode Island	Roger Williams	1636	for freedom of religion
A Town in Rhode Island	Anne Hutchinson	1638	for freedom of religion
Maryland	Catholics	1634	for freedom of religion
Pennsylvania	William Penn	1681	for freedom of religion
Georgia	James Oglethorpe	1733	to help people with little money

1. Who started the colony in Providence, Rhode Island? _____

_____

2. When was the Pennsylvania colony started? _____

3. What colony did James Oglethorpe start? _____

4. When did Anne Hutchinson start a colony? _____

5. Why did Catholics start the Maryland colony? _____

_____

6. Which colony was started to help people with little money? _____

_____

7. Which colony was started first? _____

Reading a Historical Map ★ A historical map shows how an area used to look. The historical map on this page shows the thirteen English colonies in the year 1753.

A number has been placed next to each colony on the map. Write the name of the colony on the blank line that matches the number of the colony on the map. The first one is done for you.

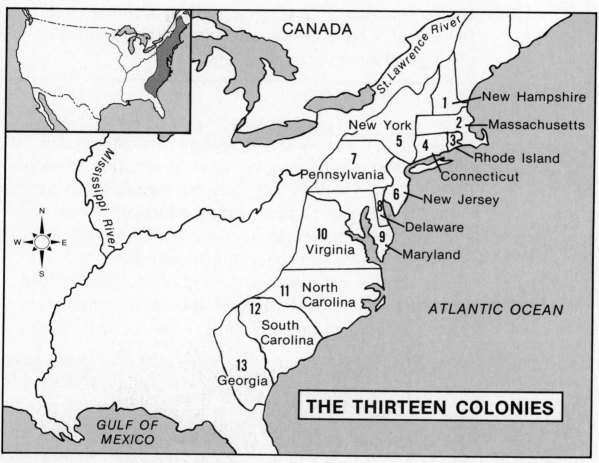

1. <u>New Hampshire</u>

2. _____

3. _____

4. _____

5. _____

6. _____

7. _____

8. _____

9. _____

10. _____

11. _____

12. _____

13. _____

CHAPTER 6

The French Come to America

New Words ☆ earn ★ French ★ shortcut ★
Jacques Cartier ★ Canada ★ St. Lawrence River ★
France ★ La Salle ★ explorer ★ body of water ★
Gulf of Mexico ★ Louisiana ★ King Louis ★
St. Louis ★ New Orleans ★ fur ★ traded ★
George Washington

A FRENCH SHIP

Many English people came to America for freedom of religion. Many poor people came to America to work hard and earn money. We learned that Spanish people came to America to find gold. The French were another group of people who came to America. Why do you think the French came to America?

The French king wanted to find a shortcut to Asia. In 1534 the king sent Jacques Cartier to America. Cartier wanted to find a river in America that he could

La Salle said that all the land around the Mississippi River would be called Louisiana.

follow west all the way to Asia. Cartier sailed to Canada. Cartier could not find a river that went to Asia. He discovered the St. Lawrence River. Look at the map on this page. Find the St. Lawrence River. Cartier said that all the land around the St. Lawrence River belonged to France. He returned to France.

La Salle was another French explorer. An explorer looks for new land. He came to America to find new land for France. In 1682 La Salle sailed from the St. Lawrence River to the Mississippi River. Then he sailed down the Mississippi River to the South of the United States. In the South, there is a body of water called the Gulf of Mexico. La Salle was the first person we know of to sail all the way down the Mississippi River to the Gulf of Mexico.

La Salle called the land near the Mississippi River "Louisiana." He put a big cross and a French flag on the land of Louisiana. La Salle said, "All the land around the Mississippi River belongs to King Louis of France. I am calling this land 'Louisiana.'" The land around the Mississippi River and the land around the St. Lawrence River belonged to France.

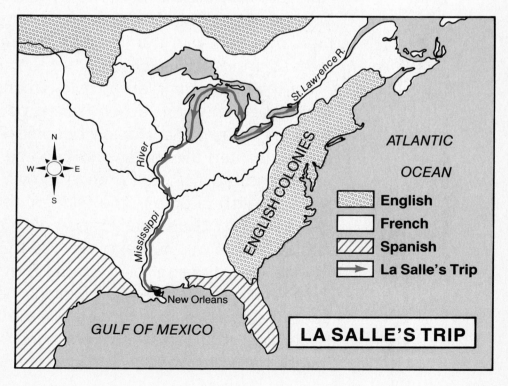

LA SALLE'S TRIP

The new village of St. Louis was built where two great rivers come together.

FRENCH SOLDIER

ENGLISH SOLDIER

The French king sent more people to America. The French started two cities on the Mississippi River. St. Louis and New Orleans were two French cities on the Mississippi. New Orleans was near the Gulf of Mexico.

The French did not build many farms and towns in America. The French came to America to find furs. The Indians hunted many animals for their furs. The French traded with the Indians for furs. In France, they sold these furs for a lot of money.

Many French people came to America to find furs and to become rich. Other French people came to America to help the Indians become Catholics. French priests wanted the Indians to become Catholics.

England did not want France to own land in America. Many English people in the thirteen colonies wanted to move west to Louisiana. France did not want English people to live in Louisiana. By 1754 England and France were fighting in America. This war was called the French and Indian War. Indians helped both sides fight. George Washington lived in the Virginia colony. He helped the English soldiers fight. The soldiers fought for many years.

Often Indians would bring animal furs to the French towns to trade.

The war ended in 1763. France lost the French and Indian War. England won the war. After the war, England owned Canada. England owned all the land that was east of the Mississippi River. Spain owned the land that was west of the Mississippi. St. Louis and New Orleans belonged to Spain. France lost all her land in America. In 1763 England and Spain owned almost all the land in America.

USING WHAT YOU'VE LEARNED

★ Read and Remember

Finish the Sentence ★ Draw a circle around the word or words that finish each sentence.

1. Jacques Cartier discovered the _____ River.

    St. Lawrence   Mississippi   Hudson

2. La Salle sailed down the _____ River to the Gulf of Mexico.

    St. Lawrence   Mississippi   Hudson

3. The French traded with the Indians for _____.

    gold   ships   furs

4. The _____ lost the French and Indian War.

   Spanish   French   Indians

5. Some French people wanted the Indians to become _____.

   Catholics   farmers   settlers

6. La Salle called the land around the Mississippi River _____.

   Spain   Louisiana   Mississippi

7. After the French and Indian War, New Orleans belonged to _____.

   Spain   Italy   France

★ Think and Apply

Cause and Effect ⋆ Read each pair of sentences. Put a **C** next to the sentence that tells a cause. Put an **E** next to the sentence that tells an effect.

1. _____   The French king wanted a shortcut to Asia.

   _____   The French king sent Cartier to America.

2. _____   Cartier returned to France.

   _____   Cartier did not find a river to Asia.

3. _____   The French did not build many farms.

   _____   The French came to America to find fur.

4. _____   England and France began to fight.

   _____   England did not want France to own land in America.

5. _____   France lost all her land in America.

   _____   France lost the French and Indian War.

6. _____   England won the French and Indian War.

   _____   England owned Canada and the land east of the Mississippi.

34

★ Skill Builder

Using Map Directions ★ In Chapter 2 you learned that there are four main directions on a map. They are north, south, east, and west. A compass rose also shows four in-between directions. They are **northeast**, **southeast**, **northwest**, and **southwest**. Southeast is between south and east. Southwest is between south and west. Sometimes the in-between directions are shortened to **NE**, **SE**, **NW**, and **SW**.

Write the shortened in-between directions on the compass rose below. One in-between direction is done for you.

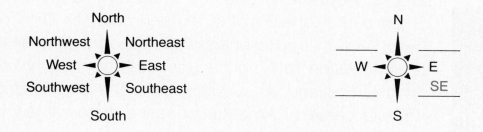

Look back at the map on page 31. Then circle the word that finishes each sentence.

1. The St. Lawrence River is in the _____.

   northeast   northwest   southwest

2. The English colonies were in the _____.

   northwest   southwest   east

3. The Mississippi River was _____ of the English colonies.

   south   west   east

4. Florida is in the _____.

   southeast   northeast   northwest

5. The Atlantic Ocean was to the _____ of the English colonies.

   north   south   east

6. New Orleans is in the _____.

   east   north   south

CHAPTER 7

Americans Fight for Freedom

New Words ☆ Americans ★ nation ★ ruled ★ King George ★ tax ★ tea ★ Boston ★ Boston Tea Party ★ disliked ★ angry ★ American Revolution

KING GEORGE III OF ENGLAND

Many people from England came to live in America. They came to live in the thirteen colonies. The people who lived in the colonies were called Americans. People came to America because they did not like the king of England. They did not like the laws in England. People came to America because they wanted more freedom.

America was not a free nation. England ruled the thirteen colonies. The king of England was also the king of the thirteen colonies. From 1760 to 1820, George III was the king of England.

Americans did not like many English laws.

36

In 1765 England made a new law. The law said that Americans had to send some of their money to England. The money that Americans sent to England was called tax money.

The Americans did not like the new tax law. They said the new law was not fair. The Americans did not want England to make tax laws for the colonies. Most people in the colonies thought that Americans should make their own laws. Some Americans decided not to pay the new taxes.

England made many laws for the American colonies. Americans did not like the English laws. In England, the English people helped make their own laws. Americans wanted to help write their own laws, too. England would not let Americans write their own laws.

In 1773 England made another law. This law said that Americans must pay a tea tax. This meant that Americans had to pay a new tax for their tea.

At the Boston Tea Party, Americans dressed as Indians and threw the English tea into the ocean.

The Americans decided to fight England to become a free country. This war is called the American Revolution.

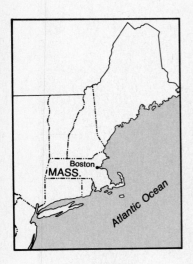

MASSACHUSETTS

Americans had to send the tax money to England. Did Americans help make this law? Americans were very angry because they did not help write the tea tax law.

Boston was a large city in Massachusetts near the Atlantic Ocean. Ships with lots of tea came to Boston. The Americans did not want to pay a tea tax. They did not want the tea. They wanted to send the tea ships back to England. England said that Americans must pay for the tea.

Some Americans decided to throw the tea into the ocean. One night in 1773, they put on Indian clothes. They went to the tea ships in Boston. The Americans threw all the tea into the Atlantic Ocean. This is known as the Boston Tea Party. The Boston Tea Party made King George very angry. He sent many English soldiers to Massachusetts.

England then made another law that Americans disliked. This law said that Americans must let English soldiers eat and sleep in their homes. The soldiers paid the Americans when they ate and slept in their homes. But Americans disliked the English soldiers. They did not want English soldiers in their homes. Americans were becoming very angry.

The angry Americans started an army. In 1775 American soldiers began to fight England for freedom. Americans wanted the same freedom that people had in England. They wanted the freedom to write their own laws. A war had started between England and America in 1775. Americans called their war the American Revolution.

USING WHAT YOU'VE LEARNED

★ Read and Remember

Write the Answer ★ Write a sentence to answer each question.

1. Who was the king of England from 1760 to 1820?

_____

_____

2. What new law did England make in 1765 that made the Americans

unhappy? _____

_____

3. What did Americans do at the Boston Tea Party?

_____

_____

4. Where did King George send soldiers after the Boston Tea Party?

_____

5. Why did American soldiers begin to fight England? _____

_____

6. When did the war between America and England begin? _____

_____

7. What did the Americans call the war between England and

America? _____

_____

★ Think and Apply

Find the Relationship ★ Read each fact below. Then look in the box for an event that is related to that fact. Write the letter of the related event on the blank.

_____ 1. Americans did not want to pay the tea tax.

_____ 2. Americans wanted more freedom.

_____ 3. King George was angry after the Boston Tea Party.

_____ 4. Americans wanted to make their own laws.

_____ 5. England won the French and Indian War.

---

a. France lost all land in America in 1763.
b. Americans didn't want England to make tax laws for the Colonies.
c. Americans threw English tea into the ocean.
d. King George sent many English soldiers to Massachusetts.
e. Americans began to fight against England.

★ Skill Builder

Reading a Time Line ★ A time line is a drawing that shows years on a line. Look at this time line. Read the time line from left to right.

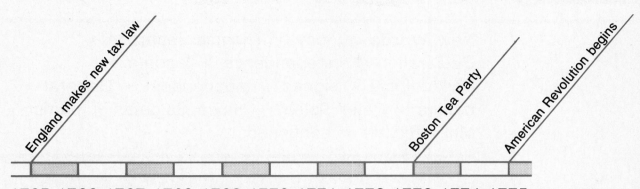

The year 1765 comes before 1766, and 1767 comes after 1766.

1. What year comes after 1774? _____

2. What year comes before 1775? _____

Events are sometimes placed on time lines. Read the events on the time line. Then answer each question.

3. When did England make a new tax law? _____

4. When was the Boston Tea Party? _____

5. When did the American Revolution begin? _____

★ Writing Workshop

What would you do if you were an American living in the thirteen colonies in 1775? Would you help the Americans or King George? Write three or four sentences that tell what you would do and why.

_____

_____

_____

_____

CHAPTER 8
A New Country Is Born

New Words ☆ obey ★ Thomas Jefferson ★ Declaration of Independence ★ leaders ★ Philadelphia ★ signed ★ independent ★ General ★ battles ★ Peter Salem ★ Haym Salomon ★ patriot ★ Molly Pitcher ★ continued

THOMAS JEFFERSON

The American Revolution began in the year 1775. At first, Americans were fighting England because they wanted more freedom. They wanted the freedom to write their own laws. In 1776 many Americans decided that they wanted America to be a free country. These people said, "England should not rule America. We do not want to obey the king of England."

Americans decided to tell the world that America no longer belonged to England. In 1776 Thomas Jefferson and a few others were asked to write the Declaration

Several people helped Thomas Jefferson (far left) write the Declaration of Independence.

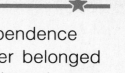

of Independence. The Declaration of Independence was a paper. It said that America no longer belonged to England. It also said that Americans did not have to obey King George. The Declaration of Independence said that the thirteen colonies were a free nation.

The leaders of the thirteen colonies went to Philadelphia. Philadelphia was a big city. It was in the Pennsylvania colony. Find Pennsylvania on the map on page 29. On July 4, 1776, the leaders signed the Declaration of Independence in Philadelphia.

England did not want America to be independent. Independent means "to be free." English soldiers continued to fight against the Americans.

George Washington was the leader of the American army. The soldiers called him General Washington. George Washington was a good leader. He tried to be fair to the soldiers, and he was a good fighter. The Americans lost many battles, or fights, but General Washington did not give up. The Americans continued to fight for independence.

GEORGE WASHINGTON

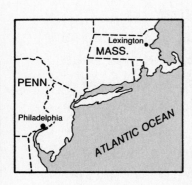

EASTERN COLONIES

The first battle of the American Revolution was at Lexington in Massachusetts. Here the Americans fought the English soldiers.

Molly Pitcher helped the American soldiers.

PETER SALEM

HAYM SALOMON

Many people tried to help America win the American Revolution. France sent French soldiers to America. French soldiers helped Americans fight against the English. There were many black people in the thirteen colonies. About five thousand blacks fought against the English army. Peter Salem was one brave black soldier. Peter Salem fought the English in Massachusetts.

Haym Salomon was a Jewish American who helped his country. The American army had little money. The soldiers did not have enough food, clothes, or guns. Some soldiers did not even have shoes. The American army needed money. Haym Salomon was a sick man, and he could not fight. But he was a rich man. He gave much of his money to the American army. The soldiers bought food, guns, shoes, and clothes with this money. Haym Salomon was a patriot. He was happy because his money helped the American army win.

Women also helped America win. Molly Pitcher helped the American soldiers. She brought water to them when they were fighting. Molly's husband, John, was a soldier. One day John was hurt during a battle. He could not fight. Molly took John's gun and shot at the English soldiers.

Americans continued to fight for eight years. The American Revolution ended in 1783. America had won.

England lost the American Revolution. When the war was over, the king of England was no longer the king of America. The thirteen colonies were a free country. Now the thirteen colonies were called thirteen states. The Americans called their free country the United States of America.

USING WHAT YOU'VE LEARNED

★ Read and Remember

Finish the Sentence ★ Draw a circle around the word or words that finish each sentence.

1. Americans told the world they were a free nation in _____.

   1765   1976   1776

2. _____ wrote the Declaration of Independence.

   George Washington   Thomas Jefferson   Peter Salem

3. Americans signed the Declaration of Independence in _____.

   Boston   Philadelphia   Jamestown

4. _____ was the leader of the American army.

   George Washington   Haym Salomon   Thomas Jefferson

5. _____ soldiers helped the Americans fight.

   Indian   French   Spanish

6. About _____ blacks fought against England.

   5,000   200   50,000

7. _____ was a brave black soldier.

   Haym Salomon   Peter Salem   Thomas Jefferson

8. _____ gave a lot of money to the American army.

   George Washington   Haym Salomon   Molly Pitcher

9. _____ fought in her husband's place.

   Peter Salem   Molly Pitcher   Haym Salomon

10. The American Revolution ended in _____.

   1765   1776   1783

★ Think and Apply

Drawing Conclusions ⋆ Read each sentence. Look for clues in the sentence to help you decide who might have said it. Draw a line from the sentence to the person who might have said it.

1. "The only way I can help is to give money."   Thomas Jefferson

2. "What I have written will tell the world we want independence."   George Washington

3. "I will fight the English in Massachusetts."   Peter Salem

4. "I'm going to lead the American army until we win this war."   Haym Salomon

5. "I'll take over since John can't keep fighting!"   Molly Pitcher

Find the Relationship ⋆ Read each fact below. Then look in the box for an event that is related to that fact. Write the letter of the related event on the blank.

_____ 1. Thomas Jefferson wanted to tell the world that the thirteen colonies were a free nation.

_____ 2. The American army needed a good leader.

_____ 3. Americans did not want to be ruled by England.

_____ 4. England did not want America to be a free country.

_____ 5. America won the Revolution and became a free country.

---

a. Americans wanted to become a free country.
b. Thomas Jefferson wrote the Declaration of Independence.
c. George Washington led the American army.
d. The English fought against the Americans.
e. England didn't rule America after the American Revolution.

★ Writing Workshop

Read about George Washington, Peter Salem, Haym Salomon, and Molly Pitcher again. Tell who you would most like to know and why. Write four or five sentences.

_____

_____

_____

_____

_____

_____

_____

_____

CHAPTER 9

The Constitution

New Words ☆ Constitution ★ vote ★ government ★
elect ★ president ★ Capitol ★ Senate ★
House of Representatives ★ senators ★
representatives ★ provides ★ Supreme Court ★
judges ★ amendments ★ Bill of Rights

THE CONSTITUTION

The American Revolution was won in 1783. The United
States was now an independent country with thirteen
states. The new country needed new laws. A
constitution is a group of laws. The leaders of the
United States decided to write laws, or a constitution,
for their new country. In 1787 leaders from twelve of
the states went to Philadelphia. In Philadelphia, the
leaders wrote the United States Constitution.

Before the American Revolution, England made laws
for the American colonies. Americans always wanted to

The American leaders talked many days about the way the
Constitution was to be written.

make their own laws. The United States Constitution says that Americans can help write their own laws. How do Americans do this?

The Constitution says that Americans should choose, or vote for, people to work for them in their government. Americans elect a president every four years. The president is the leader of the United States government. The president helps make our laws. Our laws are made in the Capitol building. The Senate and the House of Representatives are both in the Capitol building.

Men and women who write laws are called senators and representatives. Every state sends two senators to work in the Senate. States with many people send many representatives to work in the House of Representatives. States with fewer people send fewer representatives to work in the House of Representatives. The Constitution says that Americans should vote for people to be their senators and representatives. Americans help write their own laws by voting for their senators, representatives, and president.

Both the Senate and the House of Representatives meet in the United States Capitol building.

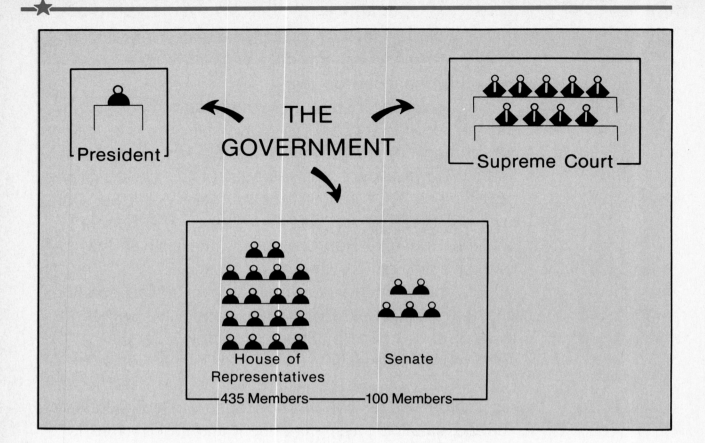

THE GOVERNMENT

President

Supreme Court

House of
Representatives
435 Members

Senate
100 Members

U.S. SUPREME COURT

The Constitution provides the United States with a Supreme Court. Judges work in the Supreme Court. In the Supreme Court, judges decide whether new laws are right or wrong. The senators and representatives must change laws that are wrong.

The Constitution was written in 1787. Since 1787, 26 amendments were added to the Constitution. An amendment is a new law in the Constitution. We can continue to add amendments, or new laws, to the Constitution.

Some of our leaders were not happy with the Constitution in 1787. The Constitution did not say that Americans had freedom of religion. The Constitution did not say that Americans had freedom of the press. "Freedom of the press" means that the government cannot tell people what they can say in newspapers and books. English soldiers had often stayed in American homes. Americans wanted a law that said the soldiers would no longer sleep in American homes.

In 1791 our leaders added ten amendments to the Constitution. These ten amendments are called the Bill of Rights. The Bill of Rights is now part of our Constitution. What are some of these rights? Every American has freedom of religion. Every American has freedom of the press. Americans do not have to let soldiers sleep in their homes. The Bill of Rights gives every American many freedoms.

Today our Constitution is more than 200 years old. The leaders of 1787 gave us good laws. These laws helped America become a great country.

USING WHAT YOU'VE LEARNED

★ Read and Remember

Finish Up ★ Choose a word in dark print to finish each sentence. Write the word on the correct blank.

vote   many   Freedom of the press   two

1. Every state sends _____ senators to work in the Senate.

2. Some states send _____ representatives to work in the House of Representatives.

3. Americans _____ for their senators, representatives, and president.

4. _____ means the government cannot tell people what they can say in newspapers and books.

Write the Answer ★ Write a sentence to answer each question.

1. Where did Americans write the Constitution? _____

_____

2. What do judges in the Supreme Court do? _____

_____

3. Why did the leaders add the Bill of Rights to the Constitution?

_____

4. What are some of the rights that the Bill of Rights added to the

Constitution? _____

_____

★ Think and Apply

Finding the Main Idea ★ Read each group of sentences below. One of the sentences is a main idea. Two sentences support the main idea. Write an **M** next to the sentence that is the main idea in each group.

1. _____ Americans were angry when they had to obey England.

_____ Americans made a constitution that says they can write their own laws.

_____ Americans wanted to make their own laws.

2. _____ The Constitution says Americans can choose people to work in their government.

_____ Americans vote for their senators and representatives.

_____ Americans vote for their president every four years.

3. _____ The Constitution did not say that Americans had freedom of speech.

_____ In 1791, America's leaders added ten amendments to the Constitution.

_____ The Constitution did not say that Americans had freedom of religion.

4. _____ The President and the Supreme Court are two parts of the government.

_____ The Senate and the House of Representatives make up one part of the government.

_____ The United States government has three parts.

★ Think and Apply

Fact or Opinion ★ A **fact** is a true statement. An **opinion** is a statement that tells what a person thinks.

> FACT = The president is elected.
> OPINION = Our president is an excellent leader.

Write **F** next to each fact below. Write **O** next to each opinion. You should find three sentences that are opinions.

_____ 1. The Constitution was written in 1787.

_____ 2. Since 1787, the Constitution has had 26 amendments added to it.

_____ 3. Our nation needs a better Constitution.

_____ 4. The men and women who write our laws are called senators and representatives.

_____ 5. Senators work harder than the president.

_____ 6. The Bill of Rights has ten amendments.

_____ 7. The Bill of Rights gives every American freedom of religion and freedom of the press.

_____ 8. It is easy to be a Supreme Court judge.

★ Skill Builder

Reading a Diagram ★ A **diagram** is a picture that helps you understand something. The diagram on page 50 helps you understand our government. Look back at the diagram. Then finish each sentence with a word in dark print.

president   representatives   nine   three

1. The United States government has _____ parts.

2. The government has one _____.

3. The government has _____ Supreme Court judges.

4. There are more _____ than senators.

CHAPTER 10 Ben Franklin

BEN FRANKLIN

Ben Franklin was born in Boston, Massachusetts, in 1706. Ben's family was very large. He had 16 brothers and sisters. In those days, there were no electric lights. People used candles to light their homes. Ben's father earned money by making soap and candles. The family was very poor.

Ben was a smart boy. He loved to read books. Ben went to school until he was 10 years old. Then Ben

When Ben was a young man, he worked in his brother's printing shop.

made soap and candles with his father. He had to help his poor family.

Ben had an older brother named James. James owned a printing shop. When Ben was 12 years old, he went to work for James. Ben became a printer. Ben and James published a newspaper together. Ben enjoyed his work, but he did not like working with James. James and Ben did not get along very well. Ben decided to run away from Boston.

Ben ran away. He went to Philadelphia. Ben worked in a printing shop in Philadelphia. When Ben was 24 years old, he published his own newspaper. People read Ben's newspaper in all 13 American colonies.

Ben wanted Philadelphia to be a better city. Ben started the first hospital in the city. He started a fire department in the city. He started a school in Philadelphia. Ben loved to read books. He knew that other people wanted to read books, too. He started Philadelphia's first public library.

Ben showed that lightning is electricity.

Benjamin Franklin helped write the Declaration of Independence. Here the declaration is being signed.

Ben knew there was something called electricity. He wanted to learn more about electricity. One night there was rain and lightning outside. Ben tied a key to the end of a kite string. He flew the kite outside. Lightning hit the kite. Electric sparks jumped off the key. Then Ben knew that lightning is electricity. People read about Ben's work in electricity all over America and Europe. Ben became famous.

Ben wanted the American colonies to become an independent country. He helped Thomas Jefferson write the Declaration of Independence in 1776. Ben was one of the men who signed the declaration. Ben wanted to help his country win the American Revolution. He was then 70 years old. He was too old to be a soldier. Ben went to France. He asked the French people to help the Americans fight. The French people liked Ben Franklin. France sent soldiers and ships to the American colonies. France helped the Americans win the war.

In 1787 Ben was 81 years old. He had another job to do. He had to help write new laws for the United States. Ben helped write the Constitution. Ben and the

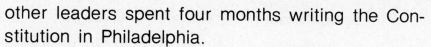

other leaders spent four months writing the Constitution in Philadelphia.

Ben died in Philadelphia when he was 84 years old. He was a very famous American. He helped Philadelphia become a great city, and he helped the United States become a free country.

USING WHAT YOU'VE LEARNED

★ Read and Remember

Match Up ★ Finish each sentence in group A with words from group B. Write the letter of the correct answer on the blank line. The first one is done for you.

GROUP A

1. Ben Franklin learned that lightning is __e__.

2. Ben helped Thomas Jefferson write the _____.

3. Ben asked _____ to help Americans fight.

4. Ben published his own _____.

5. In 1787 Ben helped write the _____.

6. Ben went to France when he was _____.

GROUP B

a. Constitution

b. 70 years old

c. newspaper

d. Declaration of Independence

e. electricity

f. France

★ Think and Apply

Cause and Effect ★ Read each pair of sentences. Write a **C** next to the sentence that tells a cause. Write an **E** next to the sentence that tells an effect.

1. _____ James and Ben did not get along very well.

_____ Ben ran away to Philadelphia.

2. _____ In Boston, Ben learned to be a printer.

_____ In Philadelphia, Ben found a job in a printing shop.

3. _____ Ben started a public library.

_____ Ben knew people liked to read books.

4. _____ Lightning hit Ben's kite and sparks flew off the key.

_____ Ben learned that lightning is a kind of electricity.

5. _____ Ben went to France to ask for help.

_____ Ben wanted to help America win the Revolution.

★ Skill Builder

Reading a Time Line ★ This time line shows important events in Ben Franklin's life. Read the events on the time line. Then answer the questions. Write **before** or **after** on the blank. The first one is done for you.

Ben is born | Ben becomes a printer | Ben runs away to Philadelphia | Ben discovers electricity | Ben goes to France | Ben helps write the Constitution

1700 1710 1720 1730 1740 1750 1760 1770 1780 1790

1. Ben Franklin became a printer _____before_____ he ran away to Philadelphia.

2. Ben ran away to Philadelphia _____ he discovered electricity.

3. Ben helped write the Constitution _____ he discovered electricity.

4. Ben went to France _____ he helped write the Constitution.

5. Ben went to France _____ he became a printer.

★ Crossword Puzzle

Each sentence below has a word missing. Choose the missing word for each sentence from the words in dark print. Then write the words in the right places on the puzzle.

ACROSS

library   kite
candles   Philadelphia

1. People can read books in a public _____.

2. Ben flew a _____ outside during a lightning storm.

3. Ben ran away from Boston to _____.

4. Ben helped his father make soap and _____.

DOWN

James   published
Boston   hospital

5. Ben and James were printers in _____.

6. Ben started a _____ for sick people.

7. _____ was Ben's older brother.

8. Ben _____ his own newspaper in Philadelphia.

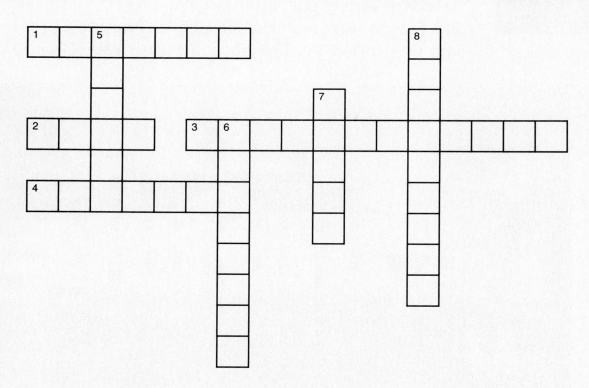

CHAPTER 11 George Washington

New Words ☆ parents ★ manage ★ wealthy ★ Martha ★ Mt. Vernon ★ commander-in-chief ★ Trenton ★ surrendered ★ Yorktown ★ capital ★ Pierre L'Enfant ★ plan ★ Benjamin Banneker

GEORGE WASHINGTON

George Washington was born in the Virginia colony on February 22, 1732. George's parents owned a large house with a lot of farm land. George loved to ride horses. He was a quiet boy. George's father died when George was 11 years old. George then helped his mother manage the family farm. He learned how to be a good farmer.

George was a soldier in Virginia. By 1754 England and France were fighting for land in America. This fight was called the French and Indian War. George

George and Martha lived in their Virginia home for many years. They called it Mt. Vernon.

became a leader of the Virginia army. He was 22 years old. George and the Americans helped the English win.

In 1759 George married a wealthy young woman named Martha. George and Martha Washington lived in a large, beautiful house in Virginia. They called their home Mt. Vernon.

MARTHA WASHINGTON

George wanted the American colonies to become a free country. He became the commander-in-chief of the American army. This means that he was the leader of all the American soldiers. The soldiers called him General Washington. George worked very hard during the American Revolution, but he did not want to be paid for his work. George did not take money for being commander-in-chief.

George lost a battle in New York City. But, he did not give up. He took his army south to Pennsylvania. On Christmas 1776, George took his army to Trenton, New Jersey. Find New Jersey on the map on page 29. George knew that the English army would not be

George Washington was the leader of the American army. He is shown here during the cold winter with his soldiers.

Washington helped plan the new capital city. But it was not ready to live in for many years. Later the city was named for him.

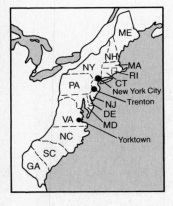

IMPORTANT BATTLES OF THE AMERICAN REVOLUTION

ready to fight. The English army was having a Christmas party. George and the Americans surprised the English army. The English army surrendered. General Washington won the battle at Trenton, but the war was not over.

The English and Americans continued to fight. The American army did not have enough food, clothes, or guns. Many soldiers became sick during the cold winters. Most soldiers liked George Washington. They stayed with him and helped him fight for American freedom.

In 1781 the Americans won an important battle in Yorktown, Virginia. Many English soldiers surrendered to George Washington in Yorktown. The Revolution ended in 1783. George went home to Mt. Vernon.

Soon the American people needed George Washington again. They wanted him to help write the Constitution. George helped write the Constitution in Philadelphia in 1787. He wanted to return to Mt. Vernon. But the United States needed a president.

Americans voted for George Washington. He became our first president in 1789. The government of the United States was in New York City. President Washington worked there.

George wanted the United States to have a capital city. He wanted the Senate, House of Representatives, Supreme Court, and the president's house to be in the capital.

George found a beautiful place for the capital between Maryland and Virginia. The capital city is now called Washington, D.C. George asked a Frenchman named Pierre L'Enfant to make a plan of the new city. Benjamin Banneker, a black American, helped L'Enfant plan the city. The government moved to Washington, D.C., in 1800.

George Washington was president for eight years. In 1793 England and France were fighting again. France wanted American soldiers to fight against England. President Washington knew that the American army was not strong. The army was not ready to fight. He did not let Americans fight for France. George helped the United States become stronger. In 1797 George returned to Mt. Vernon. He died in 1799. George Washington was one of our greatest American leaders.

BENJAMIN BANNEKER

WASHINGTON, D.C.

USING WHAT YOU'VE LEARNED

★ **Read and Remember**

Finish the Sentence ★ Draw a circle around the word or words that finish each sentence.

1. After his father died, George Washington helped his mother _____ the family farm.

   sell   manage   buy

2. George led the Virginia army in the _____ War.

   Revolutionary   Civil   French and Indian

3. George was the _____ of the American army.

   president   commander-in-chief   captain

4. George lost a battle in _____.

   Boston   Philadelphia   New York City

5. George won a Christmas battle in _____.

   New York City   Yorktown   Trenton

6. In 1787 George helped write the _____.

   Constitution   Bill of Rights   Declaration of Independence

7. George wanted the Senate, the House of Representatives, and the president's house to be in _____.

   New York City   Philadelphia   Washington, D.C.

8. Pierre L'Enfant and _____ planned the capital city of Washington, D.C.

   Ben Franklin   Peter Salem   Benjamin Banneker

9. In 1793 _____ wanted America to help fight against England.

   France   Holland   Spain

★ **Think and Apply**

Sequencing Events ★ Write the numbers **1**, **2**, **3**, **4**, and **5** next to these sentences to show the correct order.

_____ George Washington became the first president of the United States.

_____ George was a leader of the Virginia army in the French and Indian War.

_____ George won the Battle of Trenton on Christmas in 1776.

_____ President Washington did not let Americans fight for France.

_____ George became the commander-in-chief of the American army.

★ Skill Builder

Reading a Time Line ★ Sometimes time lines show decades. A **decade** is ten years. Look at this time line.

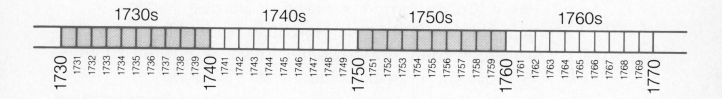

If something happened between 1730 and 1740, you say it happened in the 1730s. If something happened between 1750 and 1760, you say it happened in the _____s.

Write the decades in the boxes of the time line below. The first one is done for you. Then look at the events on the time line. Write the correct decade on the blank next to each event below.

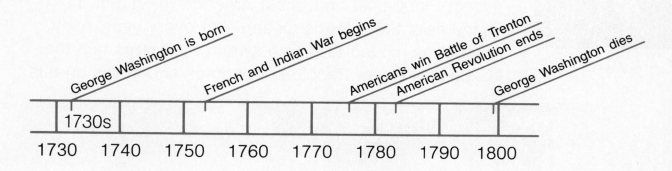

1. George Washington is born. _____

2. Americans win the Battle of Trenton. _____

3. American Revolution ends. _____

4. George Washington dies. _____

CHAPTER 12

America Doubles in Size

New Words ☆ port ★ crops ★ worried ★ allow ★ Napoleon ★ Louisiana Purchase ★ double ★ Pacific Ocean ★ Meriwether Lewis ★ William Clark ★ Sacajawea ★ Rocky Mountains ★ Oregon

THOMAS JEFFERSON

One of the men who helped write the Declaration of Independence became president of the United States in 1801. Americans voted for Thomas Jefferson to be their third president.

The American Revolution was over. The United States owned all the land east of the Mississippi River, except Florida. At first, most Americans lived in the states near the Atlantic Ocean. But every year many Americans moved to land between the states and the Mississippi River. People built homes and farms on this

New Orleans looked like this when Jefferson was president.

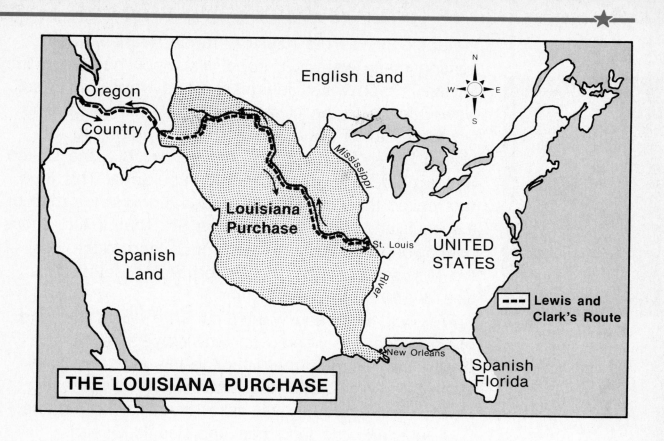

THE LOUISIANA PURCHASE

land. They were starting new states for the United States. By 1803 the United States had 16 states.

New Orleans was an important port city near the Gulf of Mexico and the Mississippi River. The American farmers sold their farm crops in New Orleans. Ships from New Orleans carried the crops to the states near the Atlantic Ocean. Other ships carried the farmers' crops to Europe.

Spain owned Louisiana and the city of New Orleans. Spain allowed American ships to sail from the port of New Orleans. In 1800 Spain gave New Orleans and Louisiana back to France. New Orleans was a French city again. President Jefferson was worried. Perhaps France would not allow Americans to use the port.

President Jefferson knew that American farmers needed the port of New Orleans. Thomas Jefferson did not want France to rule Louisiana. He wanted the United States to own New Orleans. He did not want to start a war against France. Thomas Jefferson decided to buy the city of New Orleans.

NAPOLEON OF FRANCE

Napoleon was the ruler of France. France was fighting many wars in Europe. Napoleon needed money for the French wars. Jefferson asked Napoleon to sell New Orleans to the United States. Napoleon said he would sell all of Louisiana and New Orleans to the United States for 15 million dollars. In 1803 the United States paid 15 million dollars for Louisiana. This land was called the Louisiana Purchase. Look at the map of the Louisiana Purchase on page 67. The United States now owned New Orleans and much land to the west of the Mississippi River. The United States doubled its size in 1803.

President Jefferson wanted to learn about the land of Louisiana. He wanted to know about the Indians, plants, and animals that lived on this land. He also wanted to know about the land near the Pacific Ocean. Thomas Jefferson asked two men to explore Louisiana and the land near the Pacific Ocean. Meriwether Lewis and William Clark became explorers for Thomas Jefferson.

Sacajawea was an Indian woman. She helped Lewis and Clark cross the Rocky Mountains.

Lewis and Clark started their trip across the Louisiana Purchase in 1804. They met Sacajawea. She was an Indian woman. Sacajawea said she knew how to travel across the tall Rocky Mountains in the West. Lewis and Clark wanted Sacajawea to help them cross the mountains and travel to the Pacific Ocean. Sacajawea said she would help them. She had traveled to the Pacific Ocean and knew the way.

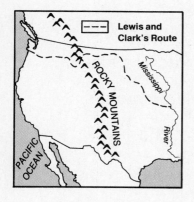

LEWIS AND CLARK'S ROUTE

Sacajawea had a little baby boy. She carried the baby on her back. She led Lewis and Clark across the Rocky Mountains. She helped them find food to eat. Lewis and Clark met Sacajawea's family. Her family gave them horses. After many months, Lewis and Clark and Sacajawea traveled through Oregon to the Pacific Ocean. The map on this page shows you the way they traveled to the Pacific Ocean. In 1806 Lewis and Clark and Sacajawea returned to their homes. They had explored 8,000 miles of land in the West.

Lewis and Clark told Thomas Jefferson about the beautiful land. They made new maps of the land in the West. Thomas Jefferson helped the United States double in size. Sacajawea and Lewis and Clark helped Americans learn about the new land they called Louisiana.

USING WHAT YOU'VE LEARNED

★ Read and Remember

True or False ★ Write **T** next to each sentence that is true. Write **F** next to each sentence that is false.

_____ 1. New Orleans always belonged to France.

_____ 2. Napoleon did not want to sell Louisiana to the United States.

_____ 3. Sacajawea, an Indian woman, led Lewis and Clark through the Rocky Mountains.

_____ 4. The Rocky Mountains are in the West.

_____ 5. Lewis and Clark and Sacajawea went to the Pacific Ocean.

_____ 6. New Orleans was an important port for American farmers.

_____ 7. Thomas Jefferson was the second president of the United States.

_____ 8. America paid $15,000 for the Louisiana Purchase.

★ Think and Apply

Cause and Effect ★ Finish each sentence in group A with an ending from group B. Write the letter next to the correct ending on the blank line. Each sentence will tell a cause and an effect.

GROUP A

1. By the year 1803, the United States had 16 states _____.

2. Americans sold their crops in New Orleans _____.

3. Thomas Jefferson bought the Louisiana Purchase _____.

4. Napoleon sold the Louisiana Purchase _____.

5. Thomas Jefferson asked Lewis and Clark to explore the land near the Pacific _____.

GROUP B

a. because he needed money to fight wars in Europe.

b. because he didn't want France to own New Orleans.

c. because many Americans had moved west of the first 13 states.

d. because ships could carry crops to Europe.

e. because he wanted to know about the land and the people in the West.

Making Comparisons ★ Read each sentence below. Decide whether it tells about Jefferson or about Napoleon. If the sentence tells about Jefferson, write a **J** before it. If the sentence tells about Napoleon, write an **N** before it.

_____ 1. He wanted to know about the land near the Pacific.

_____ 2. He needed money for many wars.

_____ 3. He wanted New Orleans for the farmers.

_____ 4. He didn't want France to own Louisiana.

_____ 5. He sold Louisiana for 15 million dollars.

★ Writing Workshop

Look at the list below. If you had gone with Lewis and Clark, which things would you have taken? Choose the five things you think are most important. Then write a sentence telling why you would have taken each one.

axe	blanket	matches
soap	candles	diary
rope	knife	animal trap

WHAT I'M TAKING   WHY I'M TAKING IT

1. _____   _____

_____

2. _____   _____

_____

3. _____   _____

_____

4. _____   _____

_____

5. _____   _____

_____

★ Crossword Puzzle

Each sentence below has a word missing. Choose the missing word for each sentence from the words in dark print. Then write the words in the right places on the puzzle.

<table>
<tr><td><u>ACROSS</u></td><td><u>DOWN</u></td></tr>
<tr>
<td>

Napoleon port
Louisiana Lewis

</td>
<td>

Jefferson France
Oregon Sacajawea

</td>
</tr>
</table>

1. The United States paid 15 million dollars for the _____ Purchase.

2. _____ and Clark explored Louisiana.

3. New Orleans is a _____ on the Gulf of Mexico.

4. _____ was the ruler of France.

5. Lewis and Clark traveled through _____ to the Pacific Ocean.

6. _____ was fighting many wars in Europe.

7. _____ helped Lewis and Clark cross the Rocky Mountains.

8. _____ wanted to buy New Orleans from France.

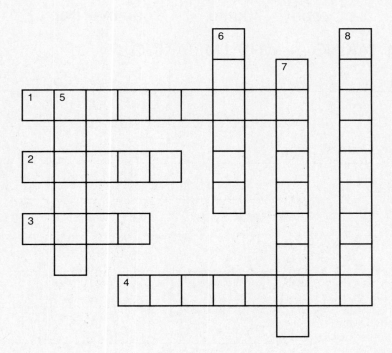

13 The War of 1812

New Words ☆ capture ★ freedom of the seas ★ angered ★ captains ★ forced ★ James Madison ★ navy ★ Dolley Madison ★ White House ★ trunk ★ burned ★ painting ★ Andrew Jackson

SHIP LANTERN

America and England were fighting again in the year 1812. Why did Americans fight a second war against England?

Napoleon, the ruler of France, started a war against England in 1803. The United States wanted to trade with both England and France. English ships captured many American ships that sailed to France. This made the United States very angry. Americans wanted freedom of the seas. "Freedom of the seas" means that ships can sail wherever they want.

England angered America in another way. English ships stopped American ships on the ocean. English captains went on the American ships. These captains

English sea captains forced American sailors to sail on English ships. The captains forced the sailors to work for England.

said that some of the Americans were really English people. They forced these Americans to sail on the English ships. They had to work for England. The English forced many Americans to work on English ships. Americans wanted to trade with France. They did not want their ships captured.

In 1812 Americans began to fight England for freedom of the seas. James Madison was the president during the War of 1812. He thought America would win the war quickly. But the American army and navy were small. The war did not end quickly. Americans fought for more than two years against England.

Americans wanted Canada to be part of the United States. American ships captured some of the lakes near Canada. The English army in Canada was strong. The United States could not capture Canada.

The American army had burned some buildings in Canada. England decided to burn the American capital city, Washington, D.C. Americans did not think England would attack their capital. There were very few

The English soldiers marched into Washington and burned the White House.

Dolley Madison asked a servant to take the painting of George Washington off the wall. The painting was wrapped in a window curtain. Then it was carried out of the White House.

DOLLEY MADISON

American soldiers in the capital. In 1814, an army of English soldiers came to Washington. They burned the Capitol building, the White House, and other government buildings.

Dolley Madison was the president's wife. She was at home in the president's house when Washington, D.C., was burning. The president's house is called the White House. President Madison was not in the city. He was with the army.

Dolley Madison was a brave lady. She did not run away from the burning city. She stayed in the White House and packed important government papers in a trunk. A beautiful painting of George Washington was in the White House. Dolley did not want the English to burn this painting. She asked someone to take it off the wall. Dolley left Washington with the painting and the government papers.

Very soon, English soldiers came to the White House and burned everything inside. Dolley Madison had saved George Washington's painting and important government papers for the United States.

ANDREW JACKSON AT THE
BATTLE OF NEW ORLEANS

England wanted to capture the city of New Orleans. Andrew Jackson was a general in the American army. He took 5,000 American soldiers to New Orleans in January 1815. General Jackson did not know that in December 1814 America and England had decided to make peace. The English army at New Orleans was very large. General Jackson and his soldiers won the Battle of New Orleans in January 1815.

In December 1814 England and America decided to stop fighting. Both countries had won and lost many battles. Both countries wanted peace. England did not win new land in the war. The United States did not win new land from the war.

Nothing really changed much because of the war. But England never again fought against the United States. England and other countries in Europe knew that the United States was now a stronger country. The United States was now strong enough to fight for what it wanted.

USING WHAT YOU'VE LEARNED

★ Read and Remember

Who Did It ★ Answer each question with the name of a person. Write a sentence about the person.

1. Who was the president during the War of 1812? _____

   _____

2. Who was the ruler of France during the War of 1812? _____

   _____

3. Who saved the painting of George Washington? _____

   _____

4. Who won the Battle of New Orleans? _____

   _____

Circle the Answer ★ Draw a circle around the correct answer.

1. What country was England fighting in 1803?

   America   France   Spain

2. What city did England burn?

   Boston   New Orleans   Washington, D.C.

3. What did England do to American ships sailing to France?

   captured them   burned them   traded with them

4. What did the Americans fight the English for in 1812?

   freedom of the seas   freedom of the press

   freedom of religion

★ Writing Workshop

It often took months for mail to get anywhere in the United States. Because of the slow mail, Andrew Jackson didn't know that the War of 1812 had ended. He and his soldiers fought the Battle of New Orleans. Imagine how he felt when he learned that there had been peace for two months. Write four or five sentences that describe his feelings.

_____

_____

_____

_____

_____

_____

_____

_____

★ Think and Apply

Drawing Conclusions ★ Read each pair of sentences. Then look in the box for the conclusion you can make. Write the letter of the conclusion on the blank.

1. English ships captured American ships.
   English captains forced American sailors to work on English ships.

   Conclusion _____

2. Americans wanted Canada to be part of the United States.
   The English army in Canada was strong.

   Conclusion _____

3. The English were burning Washington, D.C.
   Dolley Madison saved important papers and a painting.

   Conclusion _____

4. England and America wanted peace.
   Both countries had won and lost many battles.

   Conclusion _____

5. In December 1814, England and America signed a peace treaty.
   In January 1815, Jackson captured New Orleans.

   Conclusion _____

---

a. America could not capture Canada.
b. England and America signed a peace treaty.
c. Americans fought England for freedom of the seas.
d. Andrew Jackson did not know that there was peace.
e. Dolley Madison was a brave woman.

CHAPTER 14 Andrew Jackson and the Indians

New Words ☆ border ★ North Carolina ★ South Carolina ★ lawyer ★ Creek Indians ★ Cherokee Indians ★ Alabama ★ hero ★ Sequoya ★ Tennessee ★ alphabet ★ attacked ★ defeated ★ Oklahoma

ANDREW JACKSON

Andrew Jackson was born near the border between North Carolina and South Carolina in 1767. Andrew's father died before Andrew was born. His family had little money. In 1780 Andrew fought for America during the American Revolution. He was 13 years old.

Andrew's two brothers died during the American Revolution. His mother also died during the war. Andrew had to live by himself when he was only 14 years old. After the war, Andrew studied law and became a lawyer.

The leader of the Creek Indians surrendered to General Jackson.

The Cherokee newspaper was written in both English and Cherokee.

A CREEK INDIAN BOY

Andrew Jackson wanted to help his country during the War of 1812. A large group of Indians called the Creek Indians lived in the South. The Creeks helped the English soldiers fight the Americans. Andrew Jackson led his soldiers against the Creek Indians. The Americans fought the Creeks for many months.

Another group of Indians was the Cherokees. They helped Americans fight the Creek Indians. In March 1814 the Creeks lost an important battle in Alabama. They surrendered to Andrew Jackson and stopped fighting the Americans. The Creeks had to give most of their land in Alabama and Georgia to the Americans.

Andrew Jackson became a hero. People liked him because he won the battle against the Creeks and the Battle of New Orleans.

Sequoya was a Cherokee Indian who helped Americans fight the Creek Indians. Sequoya was born in Tennessee around 1760. The Cherokees had their own language. They did not know how to write the

Cherokee language. The language did not have an alphabet.

Sequoya decided to help his people learn to read and write. He carefully studied the Cherokee language. By 1821 Sequoya had made an alphabet for the Cherokee language. His alphabet had 86 letters. There was a letter for every sound in the Cherokee language.

Sequoya traveled to many Cherokee villages. He helped the Cherokees learn to read and write with his alphabet. The Cherokees started their own newspaper. It was the first Indian newspaper in America. The Cherokees started schools. Soon almost every Cherokee could read and write Sequoya's alphabet.

Indians in Florida attacked the Americans in Georgia and Alabama. Florida belonged to Spain. Andrew Jackson went to Florida. Jackson and his soldiers fought the Florida Indians and defeated them. Jackson captured part of Florida. In 1819 Spain gave Florida to the United States.

SEQUOYA AND HIS ALPHABET

Thousands of Indians moved across the country. Many died on the way.

Andrew Jackson became president of the United States in 1828. Some states did not want to obey the laws made by United States senators and representatives. The United States had tax laws. South Carolina did not want to send tax money to the government in Washington. Andrew Jackson said that all states must obey the laws of the United States. He said that he would send warships to South Carolina. South Carolina obeyed the laws. The taxes were paid.

Andrew Jackson believed that the Indians should move across the country to the West. He wanted the white people to have the Indians' land. Jackson forced the Indians to move across the Mississippi River to Oklahoma in the West. Find Oklahoma on the map on page 122.

Thousands of Indians moved across the country. Many Indians died during the long trip. The Cherokees were forced to move to Oklahoma. Sequoya also moved west. The white people were happy because they had more land. The Indians were very unhappy. They did not want to leave their homes and villages in the East.

Andrew Jackson was president for eight years. He was called the "people's president." He believed that all people, both rich and poor, should work for their country. Jackson died in 1845.

ANDREW JACKSON AS
PRESIDENT

USING WHAT YOU'VE LEARNED

★ Read and Remember

Finish the Sentence ★ Draw a circle around the word or words that finish each sentence.

1. Andrew Jackson fought in the American Revolution when he was _____ years old.

   13   15   18

2. Andrew fought against the _____ Indians during the War of 1812.

Cherokee   Creek   Florida

3. The _____ Indians fought with Jackson.

Cherokee   Creek   Florida

4. Sequoya was a Cherokee who taught his people to _____.

fight   read and write   hunt

5. _____ gave Florida to the United States in 1819.

France   England   Spain

6. _____ was a state that did not want to obey the United States' tax law.

Georgia   South Carolina   Alabama

7. President Jackson forced the Indians to move to _____.

Florida   Louisiana   Oklahoma

★ Think and Apply

Fact or Opinion ⋆ Read each sentence below. Write an **F** next to each sentence that tells a fact. Write an **O** next to each sentence that tells an opinion. You should find three opinions.

_____ 1. Andrew Jackson was a kind man.

_____ 2. Andrew Jackson fought the Creek Indians.

_____ 3. Sequoya was a Cherokee Indian.

_____ 4. Sequoya spent too much time making the alphabet.

_____ 5. The Cherokees made the first Indian newspaper in America.

_____ 6. The Cherokee newspaper had many interesting stories.

_____ 7. Jackson wanted the white people to have the Indians' land.

_____ 8. The Cherokees moved to Oklahoma.

★ Skill Builder

Interpreting a Picture ★ Pictures can help you learn about events. The picture on page 81 shows the Indians moving west. Read each pair of sentences. Circle the sentence in each pair that explains the picture on page 81. The first one is done for you.

1. The Indians were happy to move west.

   (The Indians were sad about moving west.)

2. A few Indians were forced to move west.

   Many Indians were forced to move west.

3. The Indians took animals and other things with them.

   The Indians did not take anything with them.

4. The trip was easy.

   The trip was very hard.

5. Indian people of all ages moved west.

   Only Indian adults went west.

★ Writing Workshop

Imagine that you and your family are Indians. You are forced to move west. Think about how you would feel. Write four or five sentences telling about your feelings. Be sure to tell why you feel the way you do.

_____

_____

_____

_____

_____

_____

New Words ☆ student ★ science ★ college ★ doctors ★ expensive ★ chance ★ Connecticut ★ collected ★ Mt. Holyoke Seminary ★ principal ★ subjects

MARY LYON

Mary Lyon was born in 1797. She lived on a farm in Massachusetts. There were seven children in Mary Lyon's family. All the children in the family had to help with the farm work. Mary Lyon went to school near her house. She was a smart girl and an excellent student.

Mary Lyon worked hard in school. She loved to read and learn. She decided to become a teacher. Mary Lyon became a teacher when she was 17 years old.

At that time many people thought that women were not as smart as men. Men did not think women could learn math and science. Women did not study math and science in school. Women were not allowed to go

When Mary Lyon became a teacher, there were very few women teachers. Only men could go to college.

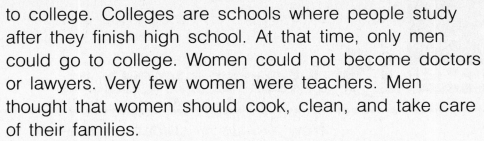

to college. Colleges are schools where people study after they finish high school. At that time, only men could go to college. Women could not become doctors or lawyers. Very few women were teachers. Men thought that women should cook, clean, and take care of their families.

Mary Lyon knew that women were as smart as men. She wanted women to have the same chance to learn that men had. Mary Lyon wanted women to go to college.

Lyon decided to start a college for women. She did not want her college to be expensive. She wanted all women to be able to study in her school. Lyon traveled through Massachusetts and Connecticut. Find Connecticut on the map on page 29. She asked people to give her money to build a college for women. Lyon collected thousands of dollars from people in Massachusetts and Connecticut. In 1836 there was enough money to start building.

Mary Lyon's college was in Massachusetts. She called it Mt. Holyoke Seminary. Mary Lyon became the

Mary Lyon called her college Mt. Holyoke Seminary.

first principal of the school. Mt. Holyoke opened in 1837. One hundred women began to study there. Some of the women were rich, but other women were poor. The women learned math, science, languages, and social studies. They studied the same subjects that men studied in college.

Mary Lyon was the principal of Mt. Holyoke for 12 years. She helped 2,000 women study there. She died in 1849. Soon more colleges for women were started in the United States. After many years, women were allowed to study in some of the colleges for men. Today Mt. Holyoke Seminary is called Mt. Holyoke College. Many women study at Mt. Holyoke every year. Mary Lyon was an important leader in women's education.

USING WHAT YOU'VE LEARNED

★ Read and Remember

Match Up ★ Finish each sentence in group A with words from group B. Write the letter of the correct answer on the blank line.

GROUP A	GROUP B
1. Women could not become _____.	a. in colleges
2. Women were not allowed to study _____.	b. Mt. Holyoke Seminary
3. The first college for women was called _____.	c. the principal
4. Lyon collected money for her school from people in _____.	d. doctors and lawyers
5. Many people did not think women were _____ as men.	e. as smart
6. Mary Lyon was _____ at Mt. Holyoke Seminary.	f. Massachusetts and Connecticut

★ Think and Apply

Sequencing Events ★ Write the numbers **1**, **2**, **3**, and **4** next to these sentences to show the correct order.

_____ Mary Lyon collected money to start a college for women.

_____ Mary Lyon became a teacher when she was 17 years old.

_____ In 1836, there was enough money to build Mt. Holyoke.

_____ Mary Lyon was Mt. Holyoke's principal for 12 years.

★ Writing Workshop

What can women do today that they could not do in 1837? Tell how women's lives have changed. Use at least three ideas from the chapter.

_____

_____

_____

_____

_____

_____

_____

_____

_____

★ Crossword Puzzle

Each sentence below has a word missing. Choose the missing word for each sentence from the words in dark print. Then write the words in the right places on the puzzle.

ACROSS

doctor   subjects   chance   languages   Massachusetts

1. Math, science, and social studies are school _____.

2. Mary Lyon wanted women to have the same _____ to learn that men had.

3. Women learned to speak different _____ at Mt. Holyoke.

4. Many years ago, a woman could not be a lawyer or a _____.

5. Mt. Holyoke was in _____.

DOWN

collected   student   farm   College   teachers

6. Mary Lyon grew up on a _____.

7. Mary Lyon was an excellent _____ in school.

8. Mary Lyon _____ money to build a college.

9. When Mary Lyon was young, few women were _____.

10. Mt. Holyoke Seminary is now called Mt. Holyoke _____.

CHAPTER 16

Texas Breaks Away From Mexico

New Words ☆ Stephen Austin ★ Texans ★ José Antonio Navarro ★ Lorenzo de Zavala ★ Santa Anna ★ fort ★ Alamo ★ Sam Houston ★ Texas Revolution ★ remember ★ San Jacinto ★ republic ★ vice president ★ break away

STEPHEN AUSTIN

Mexico and the Southwest of the United States belonged to Spain for 300 years. In 1821 Mexico became a free country. After that, Mexico ruled the Southwest of the United States. Texas is in the Southwest. It also belonged to Mexico after 1821.

Moses Austin wanted to start a colony for Americans in Texas. He died before he could start the colony. His son, Stephen Austin, decided to carry out his father's plan to settle Texas. Mexico said that new settlers in Texas would have to obey Mexican laws.

Austin sold land to many families who wanted to move to Texas.

Santa Anna and 3,000 soldiers attacked the Alamo.

Stephen Austin started an American colony in Texas in 1821. The new settlers liked Texas. The land was very cheap. The settlers started large farms. Many Americans, along with settlers from other countries, came to Texas. Soon there were many settlers living in Texas. People from Mexico came to live in Texas. People who live in Texas are called Texans.

In 1830 Mexico made a new law. The law said that Americans could no longer come to live in Texas. Most of the settlers in Texas were Americans. The Texans did not like this law. They also disliked other Mexican laws. They did not like the tax laws. Mexican law said that settlers must be Catholic. The Texans wanted to help write laws for Texas. Mexico would not let the settlers make laws for Texas.

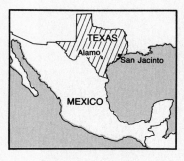

TEXAS AND MEXICO

Mexico was also angry with the new settlers. Mexico was angry because very few settlers had become Mexicans. Few Texans spoke Spanish. Many were not Catholic. Texans had decided they wanted more freedom. Mexican soldiers went to Texas to force the Texans to obey Mexican laws.

This made the Texans angry and unhappy. They did not want Mexican soldiers in Texas. Texans disliked Mexican laws. They wanted to break away from Mexico.

JOSÉ ANTONIO NAVARRO

LORENZO DE ZAVALA

The Texans decided that Texas should be independent from Mexico. In March 1836 the leaders of Texas wrote a Declaration of Independence. This Declaration said that Texas was no longer part of Mexico. The Texans said they were free.

American Texans were not the only people who wanted Texas to be free. Some Mexican Texans also worked for an independent Texas. José Antonio Navarro was a Mexican who was born in Texas. He was a friend of Stephen Austin. He signed the Texas Declaration of Independence. He later helped write a new constitution for Texas. Lorenzo de Zavala was born in Mexico. He came to live in Texas with his family. De Zavala also signed the Declaration of Independence. He told Texans to fight for their freedom.

Santa Anna, the Mexican president, would not allow the Texans to be independent. He led his army against the Texans. There were 187 Texan soldiers in a fort called the Alamo. Santa Anna and 3,000 Mexican soldiers attacked the Alamo. The Texans were brave and would not surrender. The Texans

After the battle at San Jacinto, Santa Anna was caught and was brought to Sam Houston. Houston's leg was hurt in the battle.

SUZANNA DICKENSON
ESCAPED FROM THE ALAMO

SAM HOUSTON

fought for many days. Santa Anna won the Battle of the Alamo. All 187 Texan soldiers were killed.

Sam Houston became the commander-in-chief of the Texas army. The Texans called their war against Mexico the Texas Revolution. Sam told his soldiers to fight the Mexicans. He told them to remember the brave people who died at the Alamo. On April 21, 1836, the Texans fought Santa Anna again. They fought at the San Jacinto River. "Remember the Alamo!" Sam Houston's soldiers shouted as they fought the Mexicans. The battle did not last very long. The battle was short, but the Texans won. Santa Anna surrendered to Sam Houston. Texas was now free.

Texas was no longer part of Mexico, and Texas was not part of the United States. Texas became a republic. A republic is a free country.

Texans voted for their leaders. Lorenzo de Zavala was a vice president of Texas. Sam Houston became the first president of Texas.

Texans wanted to become part of the United States. The United States was not ready for another new state.

USING WHAT YOU'VE LEARNED

★ Read and Remember

Draw a Line ★ Draw a line from the name of the person to the words that tell what the person did.

1. Stephen Austin

2. José Antonio Navarro

3. Lorenzo de Zavala

4. Sam Houston

5. Santa Anna

a. was the commander-in-chief of the Texas army.

b. was the president of Mexico.

c. helped write the Texas constitution.

d. carried out his father's plan to settle Texas.

e. was vice president of the Texas Republic.

True or False ★ Write **T** next to each sentence that is true. Write **F** next to each sentence that is false.

_____ 1. Mexico became independent from Spain in 1821.

_____ 2. José Antonio Navarro started an American colony in Texas.

_____ 3. There were more Mexicans than Americans in Texas.

_____ 4. Texans said they were free when they wrote a Declaration of Independence.

_____ 5. Texans won the Battle of the Alamo.

_____ 6. Texas became a free republic after the Texas Revolution in 1836.

★ Think and Apply

Making Comparisons ★ The Texas Revolution was fought in 1836. Before this war began, Mexico and Texas were angry with each other. Both sides had reasons to be angry. Read pages 90 to 92 again. Then write three reasons why each side was angry.

Why was Mexico angry with Texas?

1. _____

_____

2. _____

_____

3. _____

_____

Why were Texans angry with Mexico?

1. _____

_____

94

2. _____

_____

3. _____

_____

★ Writing Workshop

Read about the Texas Revolution again. Why was "Remember the Alamo" a good thing to shout at the battle near the San Jacinto River? Write a paragraph saying why. Include at least three reasons.

_____

_____

_____

_____

_____

_____

_____

_____

_____

_____

_____

17 America Grows Still Larger

New Words ☆ accept ★ Rio Grande ★ Mexican War ★ surrendered ★ peace treaty ★ citizens ★ Mexican Cession ★ Nevada ★ Utah ★ Arizona ★ Gadsden Purchase ★ railroads ★ Mexican Americans

We learned that Texans won their war against Mexico and started a free republic. Santa Anna had surrendered to the Texans. But Mexico did not accept his surrender. Texans wanted to become part of the United States. But the Mexicans said that Texas was still part of Mexico.

The Mexicans said there would be a war if Texas became part of the United States. In 1845 United States senators and representatives voted for Texas to become a state. In that year, Texas became the 28th state in the United States. The Mexicans were very

When the Texas flag was lowered, Texas became the 28th state in the United States.

American soldiers captured Mexico City, the capital city of Mexico. Here American soldiers are shown in the center of town.

angry because they lost Texas to the United States.

In 1846 a war started between the United States and Mexico. The two countries were angry. The United States said that all the land to the northeast of the Rio Grande belonged to Texas. The Rio Grande is the river that separates Texas and Mexico. Mexico said that Texas should be smaller. The Mexicans said that much land northeast of the Rio Grande belonged to Mexico.

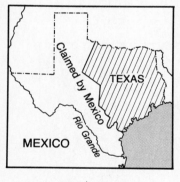

TEXAS LAND CLAIMED
BY MEXICO IN 1846

The United States and Mexico sent soldiers to the Rio Grande. The soldiers began to fight. This war was called the Mexican War. During the war, American soldiers captured California and New Mexico. The Mexican soldiers were brave. They did not stop fighting. Americans and Mexicans continued to fight. American soldiers went into Mexico. They captured Mexico City, the capital of Mexico. At last, in 1848 the Mexicans surrendered. The war was over.

The leaders of the United States and Mexico signed a peace treaty in 1848. The peace treaty said there was peace between the United States and Mexico. The treaty said that the Rio Grande was the line between Texas and Mexico. Texas, California, New Mexico, and most of the Southwest became part of the United States. The peace treaty said the United States would give Mexico 15 million dollars for this land. The treaty also said that Mexicans in the Southwest could become American citizens.

The land that the United States got in 1848 was called the Mexican Cession. California, Nevada, Utah, Arizona, and New Mexico were part of the Mexican Cession. Later, they became five new states in the United States. Find the Mexican Cession on the map on this page. The United States now owned land from the Atlantic Ocean to the Pacific Ocean.

Americans wanted a railroad across the south of the United States. The land south of the Mexican Cession was a good place for a railroad. In 1853 the United States gave Mexico 10 million dollars for the land. This land was called the Gadsden Purchase. Find the Gadsden Purchase on the map below. It is where southern Arizona and New Mexico are today. Years later, Americans built a railroad across the Gadsden Purchase.

The Mexicans in the Southwest became American citizens after the Mexican War. They were called

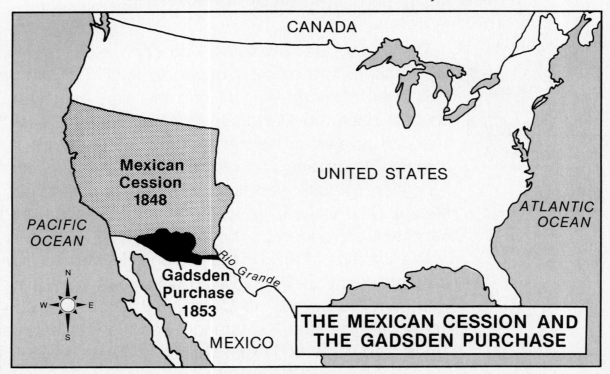

THE MEXICAN CESSION AND THE GADSDEN PURCHASE

Mexican Americans. Many Mexican Americans were not happy when Mexico lost the war in 1848. Some Mexican Americans lost part of their land in the United States.

Many Mexican Americans tried to help their new country. They helped build farms in the Southwest. They helped build railroads for the United States. They helped other Americans look for gold in the Southwest.

The land between the Atlantic Ocean and the Pacific Ocean was now American land. The United States had become a strong country with a lot of new land and many new people.

USING WHAT YOU'VE LEARNED

★ Read and Remember

Finish Up ★ Choose a word in dark print to finish each sentence. Write the word on the correct blank.

south Texas Rio Grande
Pacific Mexico New Mexico

1. In 1846 a war started between the United States and

   _____.

2. The Mexican War was fought over land in _____.

3. The peace treaty of 1848 said that the _____ was the line between Texas and Mexico.

4. After the Mexican War, the United States owned land from the

   Atlantic Ocean to the _____ Ocean.

5. Americans wanted to build a railroad across the

   _____ of the United States.

6. Parts of southern Arizona and _____ were sold as the Gadsden Purchase.

When Did It Happen ★ Write the correct date next to each question.

1. When did Texas become a state? _____

2. When did the Mexican War start? _____

3. When did Mexico lose the war? _____

4. When did Americans and Mexicans sign a peace treaty?

   _____

5. When did the United States pay 10 million dollars for the Gadsden

   Purchase? _____

★ Think and Apply

Cause and Effect ★ Read each pair of sentences. Write a **C** next to the sentence that tells a cause. Write an **E** next to the sentence that tells an effect.

1. _____ Texas became a state.

   _____ Mexico and the United States fought the Mexican War.

2. _____ Mexico surrendered in 1848.

   _____ The United States captured Mexico City.

3. _____ In 1848, the United States got land called the Mexican Cession.

   _____ California, Nevada, Utah, Arizona, and New Mexico became part of the United States.

4. _____ The United States bought the Gadsden Purchase.

   _____ The United States wanted to build a railroad across the south.

5. _____ The United States paid 10 million dollars for the Gadsden Purchase.

   _____ The United States had land to build a railroad across the South.

★ Skill Builder

Using Map Directions ★ Look back at the map on page 98. Draw a circle around the word that finishes the sentence.

1. The Gadsden Purchase is _____ of Mexico.

   east   south   north

2. The Pacific Ocean is _____ of the Mexican Cession.

   southeast   east   west

3. The Rio Grande is _____ of the Gadsden Purchase.

   south   southwest   east

4. The Mexican Cession is _____ of the Gadsden Purchase.

   south   southeast   north

5. Mexico is _____ of the United States.

   south   north   west

★ Writing Workshop

The U.S. and Mexico signed a treaty in 1848. Was the treaty better for the U.S. or for Mexico? Write a paragraph telling why.

_____

_____

_____

_____

_____

_____

_____

★ Crossword Puzzle

Each sentence below has a word missing. Choose the missing word for each sentence from the words in dark print. Then write the words in the right places on the puzzle.

ACROSS

treaty   California
railroad   Gadsden

1. _____ was part of the Mexican Cession.

2. In 1848 the United States and Mexico signed a peace _____.

3. In 1853 the United States bought the _____ Purchase.

4. Americans built a _____ across the Gadsden Purchase.

DOWN

Nevada   War
Mexican   citizens

5. The Mexican _____ started after Texas became a state.

6. Mexicans of the Southwest could become American _____.

7. _____ was part of the Mexican Cession.

8. The land that the United States got from Mexico in 1848 was the _____ Cession.

18 On to Oregon and California

New Words ☆ 1840s ★ covered wagons ★ oxen ★ wagon train ★ followed ★ Oregon Trail ★ coast ★ several ★ Idaho ★ while ★ James Marshall ★ gold rush ★ South America ★ lucky ★ factories

A COVERED WAGON

"On to Oregon! Let's move to Oregon!" said thousands of Americans in the 1840s. Oregon had lots of trees for building new houses. Oregon had good land for farming. Soon thousands of Americans moved west to build new homes and farms in the Oregon country.

The trip to Oregon was long and slow. There were no roads across the United States to Oregon. Families traveled to Oregon in covered wagons. Horses and oxen pulled the covered wagons. In 1843 many families in 120 covered wagons met in Independence,

The wagon trip to Oregon took many months. There were almost no towns along the way.

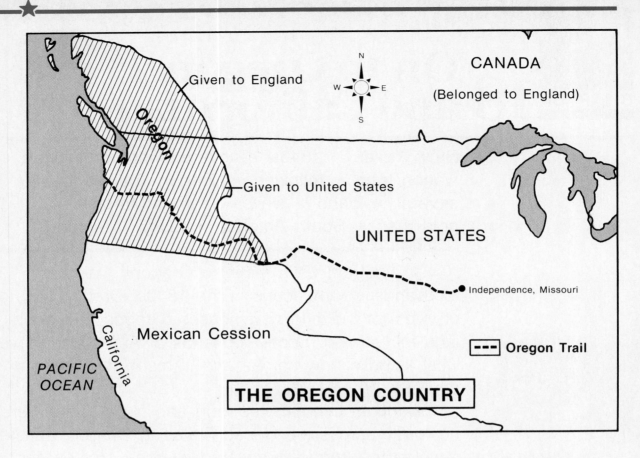

THE OREGON COUNTRY

Given to England

Oregon

Given to United States

CANADA
(Belonged to England)

UNITED STATES

Independence, Missouri

Mexican Cession

California

PACIFIC
OCEAN

- - - Oregon Trail

Missouri. These 120 covered wagons made a wagon train. The covered wagons traveled together across the Great Plains and the Rocky Mountains to Oregon. The trip took almost six months!

At last the families reached the Oregon country. They had traveled many miles. The families had followed a trail to Oregon. It became known as the Oregon Trail. Find the Oregon Trail on the map on this page. Thousands of people came to Oregon on the Oregon Trail. These people were some of the first Americans to settle along the Pacific coast.

The Oregon country was much bigger than our state of Oregon today. The Oregon country included parts of several states and part of Canada. England and the United States had shared the Oregon country for many years. The two nations could not decide on a way to divide Oregon. Many people thought England and the United States would fight for Oregon. This time the two nations did not fight. They signed a peace treaty about Oregon in 1846.

The treaty said that northern Oregon was part of Canada. Canada and northern Oregon belonged to England. Southern Oregon became part of the United States. Our states of Oregon, Washington, and Idaho were part of the Oregon country.

The United States government gave free farm land to families that moved to Oregon. Many Americans came to Oregon on the Oregon Trail for free land. In 1859 United States senators and representatives voted for Oregon to become a state.

While thousands of Americans were moving to Oregon, other Americans were rushing to California. One day in 1848, a man named James Marshall found pieces of gold in a river in California. Soon everyone knew that James Marshall had found gold.

People from all over the United States began moving to California. "Gold! Gold! Gold! There's gold in California," said Americans as they traveled to California. They wanted to find gold and become rich. We say that California had a "gold rush" in 1848 and

Many people came to California to find gold. San Francisco grew from a small, quiet town to a large, noisy city in only a year.

LOOKING FOR GOLD

1849 because thousands of people came to find gold. Some people sailed all the way around South America to go to California. Other people traveled across the United States in covered wagons to California.

Some people were lucky in California. They found gold and became rich. Most people did not find gold. Many people stayed in California. They built farms and factories. They started new cities. They built stores and houses. By 1850, 90,000 people were living in California. The United States senators and representatives voted for California to become a state in 1850.

The California gold rush brought thousands of settlers to California. The Oregon Trail brought thousands of Americans to the Northwest. Every year, more Americans moved west to California and Oregon.

USING WHAT YOU'VE LEARNED

★ Read and Remember

Finish the Sentence ★ Draw a circle around the word or words that finish each sentence.

1. Families traveled in covered wagons across _____ to Oregon.

   the Rocky Mountains   Canada   Mexico

2. Thousands of Americans went to the Oregon country in the _____.

   1820s   1830s   1840s

3. In 1843 families started a wagon train in _____ that went to Oregon.

   Idaho   Missouri   Massachusetts

4. In 1846 the northern part of the Oregon country became part of

   _____.

   the United States   Canada   Washington

5. Oregon, Washington, and _____ were part of the Oregon country.

Arizona   Idaho   Texas

6. Families that moved to Oregon were given free _____.

wagons   houses   farmland

7. In 1848 and 1849, Americans rushed to California to find _____.

silver   gold   trees

8. California became a state in _____.

1850   1859   1860

★ Think and Apply

Find the Relationship ★ Read each fact below. Then look in the box for an event that is related to that fact. Write the letter of the related event on the blank.

_____ 1. Gold was found in California.

_____ 2. There was no road to California.

_____ 3. The United States government gave free land to people who went to Oregon.

_____ 4. England and the United States decided to share the Oregon country.

_____ 5. There was no road to Oregon.

> a. The trip to Oregon was long and slow.
> b. People rushed to California.
> c. People sailed all the way around South America to get to California.
> d. The United States and England signed a treaty in 1846.
> e. Many Americans moved to Oregon.

★ Skill Builder

Reading a Historical Map ★ The map below shows how the United States became a large nation. Notice each area and when it became part of the United States.

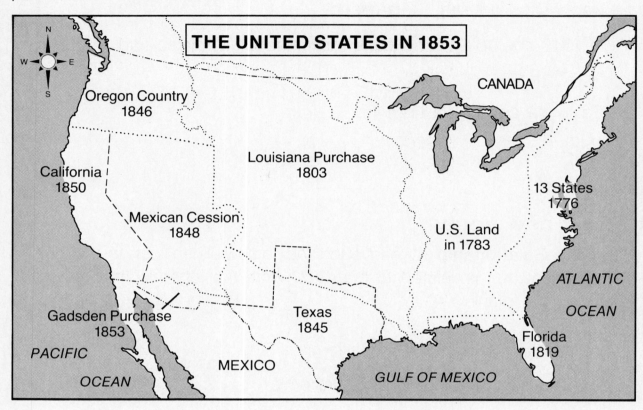

Use the map to answer each question.

1. What land did the United States get in 1776?

   Texas   First 13 States   Louisiana

2. What southeast state belonged to Spain before 1819?

   Oregon   Massachusetts   Florida

3. What land did the United States buy in 1803?

   New York   Louisiana Purchase   Texas

4. Which northwest land became part of the United States in 1846?

   Oregon   Massachusetts   Louisiana

5. Which land did the United States buy in 1853?

   Gadsden Purchase   Oregon   Texas

CHAPTER 19

The Southern States Leave

New Words ☆ quarreling ★ blacks ★ slaves ★ plantations ★ cotton ★ sugarcane ★ tobacco ★ slavery ★ Harriet Tubman ★ escape ★ products ★ Abe Lincoln ★ Confederate States of America ★ eleven

A SLAVE SALE

The United States had become a large country after the Mexican War. Things were not going well in the United States. The Northern states were quarreling with the Southern states. The Northern states were called the North, and the Southern states were called the South. Why did the North and South quarrel?

In Chapter 5, we learned how the English started colonies in America. In 1619 the English brought black people to work in America. The blacks came from Africa. Most blacks were slaves in America. A slave belongs to another person. A slave is not paid for doing work. A slave is not free.

In the South slaves did most of the farm work.

Sometimes slaves escaped and went to other places where they could be free.

At first, there were slaves in both the North and in the South. But farms were small in the North. Many people there did not need slaves to work in their farms and factories. After many years, there were few slaves in the North.

In the South, some people owned very large farms called plantations. The owners grew cotton, sugarcane, and tobacco on their plantations. Plantation owners needed many workers. They bought slaves to do the work. The owners did not pay the slaves for their work.

The farms in the North were not as large as the plantations. In the North farmers did not buy slaves. The plantation owners in the South thought they could not grow crops without slaves.

After the Mexican War, Americans moved to the West. People from the South wanted to start new plantations in the West. They wanted to bring their slaves. The Northern states did not want slavery in the West.

The North and South began to quarrel. In the North, people said that all people should be free. They said that it was not right for one person to own another person. In the South, people said that the Constitution allowed people to own slaves. People in the South said that people in the North should not tell them what to do. The people in the North wanted to make new laws against slavery in the West. This made the South very angry.

HARRIET TUBMAN

Harriet Tubman helped many slaves become free men and women. Harriet Tubman had been a slave herself. She ran away to the North. In the North, she became a free woman. She went back to the South and helped slaves escape to Canada. In Canada, the slaves were free. Harriet Tubman helped hundreds of slaves get their freedom.

The North and South were also angry about a tax law. There were many factories in the North. People made shoes, clothes, and other things in factories. There were very few factories in the South. People in the South had to buy many things from the North and from Europe. The North wanted the Southern people to pay extra money, or a tax, for everything they bought from Europe. The tax made things from Europe more

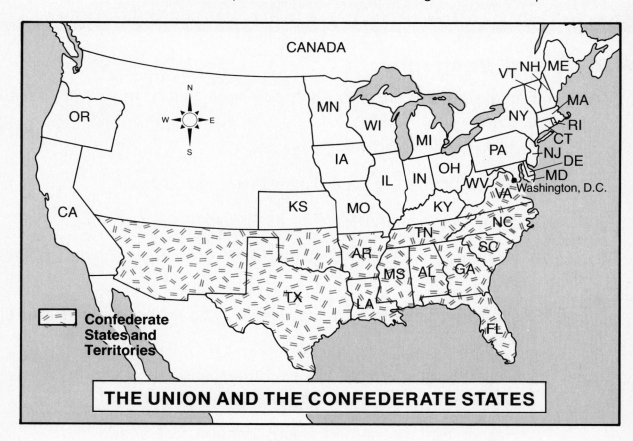

THE UNION AND THE CONFEDERATE STATES

expensive. Factories in the North also made their products more expensive. The South did not like paying more for things made in both Europe and the North.

In 1860 a man named Abe Lincoln became the president of the United States. Abe Lincoln said that slavery should not be allowed in the West. The North liked what Abe said, but the South did not.

The South decided that they no longer wanted to be part of the United States. In 1861 they started a new country. They called their country the Confederate States of America. Eleven Southern states left the United States. They became part of the new Confederate States of America.

Abe Lincoln was very unhappy. He said that the United States must be one country, not two. Would the United States and the Confederate States become one country again? Would it take a war to get them together? Chapter 20 will give you the answers.

ABE LINCOLN

USING WHAT YOU'VE LEARNED

★ Read and Remember

True or False ★ Write **T** next to each sentence that is true. Write **F** next to each sentence that is false.

_____ 1. Slaves were paid for their work.

_____ 2. Slaves worked on large plantations in the North.

_____ 3. There were many factories in the North.

_____ 4. People in the South said that the Constitution allowed people to own slaves.

_____ 5. President Lincoln said that slavery should be allowed in the West.

_____ 6. Eleven states left the United States and became the Confederate States of America.

_____ 7. Harriet Tubman helped slaves escape to Canada.

★ Think and Apply

Making Comparisons ★ Read each sentence below. Decide whether it tells about the North or the South. If the sentence tells about the North, write an **N** before it. If the sentence tells about the South, write an **S** before it.

_____ 1. There are large plantations with many slaves.

_____ 2. There are small farms with few slaves.

_____ 3. Cotton, sugarcane, and tobacco are grown on plantations.

_____ 4. Shoes and clothes are made in factories.

_____ 5. There are many factories where people are paid to work.

_____ 6. Most people said it was not right for one person to own another.

_____ 7. People believed they needed slaves to start plantations in the West.

_____ 8. People didn't like paying more for things made in northern factories.

★ Writing Workshop

In 1861 the South started the Confederate States of America. Write a paragraph to explain three reasons why the southern states started the Confederate States of America.

_____

_____

_____

_____

_____

★ Skill Builder

Reading a Bar Graph ⋆ Graphs are drawings that help you compare facts. The graph on this page is a **bar graph**. It shows facts using bars of different lengths. The bar graph below shows the number of people who lived in the United States in 1860.

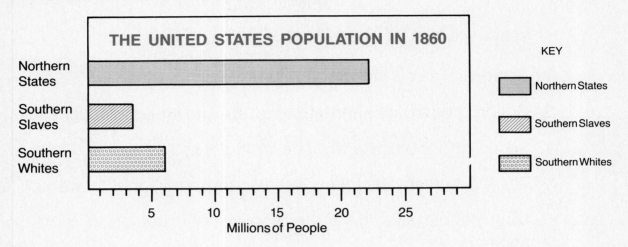

THE UNITED STATES POPULATION IN 1860

Northern States
Southern Slaves
Southern Whites
Millions of People

KEY
Northern States
Southern Slaves
Southern Whites

Use the bar graph to answer each question.

1. How many people lived in the North?

   3½ million   almost 6 million   22 million

2. How many slaves lived in the South?

   3½ million   almost 6 million   22 million

3. Which group had the largest population?

   Northern States   Southern Whites   Southern Slaves

Make a Graph ⋆ In 1863, there were 11 Confederate States. There were 24 Union States. Draw a bar for each group of states on the graph below.

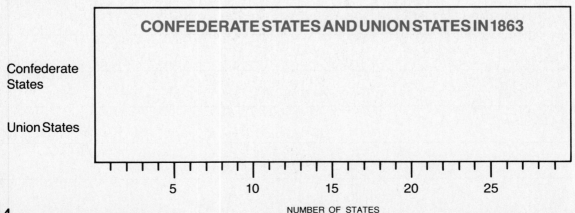

CONFEDERATE STATES AND UNION STATES IN 1863

Confederate States

Union States

NUMBER OF STATES

New Words ☆ Union ★ Fort Sumter ★ Confederates ★ Civil War ★ Confederacy ★ Robert E. Lee ★ kind ★ destroyed ★ Richmond ★ rebuild

A BUGLE USED BY A CONFEDERATE SOLDIER

The South had started a new country called the Confederate States of America. President Lincoln did not want the North to fight against the South. He wanted the South to become part of the United States again. Another name for the United States is the *Union.* The South did not want to fight against the Union. But the South did not want to be part of the Union.

The United States Army owned a fort called Fort Sumter in South Carolina. South Carolina was one of the Confederate States. People who lived in the

Fort Sumter was in South Carolina, a Confederate state. But the fort was owned by the United States Army. The Confederates attacked the fort.

115

Many people were killed in the Civil War.

ABE LINCOLN

Confederate States were called Confederates. They said that the United States must give Fort Sumter to the Confederate States of America. But Union soldiers would not surrender Fort Sumter.

In 1861 Confederate soldiers began to shoot at Fort Sumter. Then the Union soldiers surrendered the fort. A war between the Northern and Southern states had begun. We call this war the Civil War. The South fought to have their own country, the Confederate States of America. The North fought so that all states would remain part of the Union.

At first the Confederates were sure they would win. They had many good army generals and brave soldiers. But the North was stronger than the South. The North had more people and more soldiers. The North had more money to pay for a war. The North had more railroads. Union soldiers traveled on these railroads to many places. The North had more factories, too. The North made guns for war in their factories.

President Lincoln was the leader of the Union. He went to school for less than one year. He taught himself many things by reading books. He became a good leader. He wanted the North and South to become one nation again.

Abe Lincoln wanted the slaves to be free. In 1863 he gave orders that said all slaves in the Confederate States were free men and women.

Robert E. Lee was the leader of the Confederate army. Robert E. Lee loved the United States. He did not like slavery. He also loved his own state of Virginia. President Lincoln wanted Robert E. Lee to lead the Union army. Robert E. Lee would not fight against his family and friends in Virginia. Instead, he became the leader of the Confederate army. Robert E. Lee was a kind man. He was an excellent leader. He led the Confederate soldiers for four long years.

The South won many battles in the beginning of the war. Most of the Civil War battles were in the South. The fighting destroyed houses, cities, and plantations in the South. The Union soldiers captured New Orleans and other Southern cities.

In 1865 the Union soldiers captured Richmond, Virginia. Richmond was the capital of the Confederate States of America. Then Robert E. Lee knew that the Confederates could not win the war. There was very little food to eat in the South. Lee's army was hungry

ROBERT E. LEE

Many buildings were destroyed in Richmond. Richmond was the capital city of the Confederate States of America.

CONFEDERATE AND UNION
BATTLE FLAGS

and weak. He did not want more people to die in the war. Robert E. Lee surrendered in April 1865. The war was over. Plans were made to return the Confederate states to the Union. Robert E. Lee returned to Virginia. He told people in the South to help the United States become a strong country.

President Lincoln was glad that the United States had become one nation again. Abe Lincoln wanted Americans to rebuild the South. He wanted Americans in the North and South to like each other again. A few days after the Civil War ended, Abe Lincoln was shot in the head. Abe died the next day. Americans in the North and South were sad because their great leader was dead.

People in the North and South were Americans once again. Together they would continue to build a great nation in America.

USING WHAT YOU'VE LEARNED

★ Read and Remember

Write the Answer ★ Write a sentence to answer each question.

1. Why did the Confederates attack Fort Sumter? _____

_____

_____

2. Why was the North stronger than the South? (Write 2 sentences.)

_____

_____

_____

3. What order did Lincoln give in 1863? _____

_____

_____

4. When did the Civil War end? _____

_____

Finish Up ⋆ Choose a word in dark print to finish each sentence. Write the word on the correct blank.

Abraham Lincoln   **New Orleans**   **Robert E. Lee**
Fort Sumter   **Richmond**

1. _____ was the president of the Union during the Civil War.

2. The Union surrendered _____ in South Carolina.

3. _____ was the capital of the Confederate States of America.

4. The leader of the Confederate soldiers was _____.

5. Union soldiers captured _____ and Richmond.

★ **Writing Workshop**

Write about the Civil War. Tell how it began or how it ended. Write at least three sentences.

_____

_____

_____

_____

_____

_____

★ Skill Builder

Reading a Table ★ A table lists a group of facts. You can compare facts by reading tables. Look at the table below.

THE UNION AND CONFEDERACY BEFORE THE CIVIL WAR		
	UNION	CONFEDERACY
Bank money	$330,000,000	$47,000,000
Number of factories and shops	111,000	21,000
Miles of railroad track	22,000	9,000

To learn facts about the Union and the Confederacy, read the numbers listed beneath each heading. Read the chart from left to right to find out what the numbers in the table stand for. Then answer the questions.

1. How much money did the Union have? _____

_____

2. How many factories and shops did the Confederacy have?

_____

3. How many miles of railroad track did the Union have?

_____

4. Which side had less money? _____

_____

5. Which side had more factories and shops? _____

_____

★ Think and Apply

Finding the Main Idea ★ Read each group of sentences below. One of the sentences is a main idea. Two sentences support the main idea. Write an **M** next to the sentence that is the main idea.

1. _____ The South had good army generals.

   _____ The Confederates thought they would win the war.

   _____ The South had brave soldiers.

2. _____ The North had more factories than the South.

   _____ The North had more soldiers than the South.

   _____ The North was stronger than the South.

3. _____ The North and the South fought for Fort Sumter.

   _____ Fort Sumter was in one of the Confederate states.

   _____ Union soldiers would not surrender Fort Sumter.

4. _____ The Confederate capital had been captured.

   _____ The Confederates surrendered in April 1865.

   _____ The Confederate army was weak and hungry.

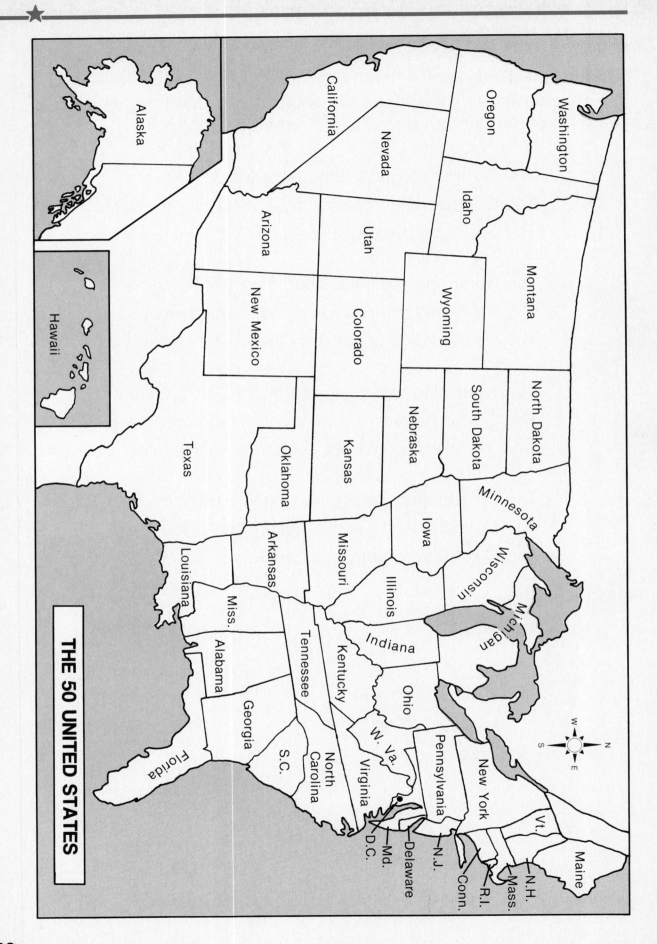

THE 50 UNITED STATES

Alaska

Hawaii

California
Oregon
Washington
Nevada
Idaho
Arizona
Utah
Montana
New Mexico
Colorado
Wyoming
Texas
Oklahoma
Kansas
Nebraska
South Dakota
North Dakota
Louisiana
Arkansas
Missouri
Iowa
Minnesota
Wisconsin
Michigan
Miss.
Alabama
Tennessee
Kentucky
Illinois
Indiana
Ohio
Georgia
S.C.
North Carolina
W. Va.
Virginia
Pennsylvania
New York
Florida
D.C.
Md.
Delaware
N.J.
Conn.
R.I.
Mass.
N.H.
Vt.
Maine

W
N
S
E

INDEX

LIST OF MAPS